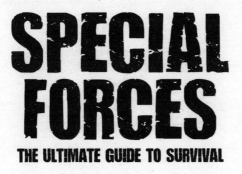

# SPECIAL FORCES

## FORCES

### THE ULTIMATE GUIDE TO SURVIVAL

HOW TO FIGHT YOUR WAY OUT
OF ANY MILITARY DISASTER

# SPECIAL FORCES

THE ULTIMATE GUIDE TO SURVIVAL

ROBERT STIRLING

JOHN BLAKE

Published by John Blake Publishing Ltd,
3 Bramber Court, 2 Bramber Road,
London W14 9PB, England

www.johnblakepublishing.co.uk

First published in hardback in 2009

ISBN: 978 1 84454 783 8

British Library Cataloguing-in-Publication Data:

A catalogue record for this book is available from the British Library.

Design by www.envydesign.co.uk

Printed in the UK by CPI William Clowes, Beccles, NR34 7TL

1 3 5 7 9 10 8 6 4 2

Papers used by John Blake Publishing are natural, recyclable products
made from wood grown in sustainable forests. The manufacturing
processes conform to the environmental regulations of the
country of origin.

This book is aimed at soldiers who understand the responsibilities and risks involved in their line of work. The publisher warns that many of the strategies and procedures herein could be dangerous or fatal if practised by untrained persons.

*Special Forces – The Ultimate Guide to Survival* is intended for information and should not be imitated by unqualified personnel. The publisher accepts no responsibility for any injury or death caused by actions taken as a result of reading the material in this book.

# Contents

# Introduction: For Those Who Choose to Go into Harm's Way

This book is written for you: the soldier, the special forces operator, the airman, the intelligence agent or the spy.

The enemies of freedom are getting stronger.

The risks you take are increasing.

This book will help bring the odds back into your favour. When you have read it I want you to feel confident you can survive and come out on top – against anyone, anywhere.

Warning: this book is about staying alive when the shit has hit the fan – your aircraft has come down hard or your team is all dead, your nearest mate is a hundred miles away and everyone around wants to kill you. It is not bedtime reading for children. Don't read this book if you are a timid sort of person. It *will* give you nightmares. What follows is written for men going into harm's way and *will* offend those of a gentle nature.

This book is not about eating bugs and mushrooms.

There are plenty of books of that sort around if you want to become a boy scout. If you are, or want to be, a soldier – particularly a special forces soldier, a special forces or secret service operator – or perform other covert jobs in trouble spots around the world, this is the book you need. It is written for those of you who *choose* to go into harm's way. You will not come to serious harm in Tesco. Harm's way is when you are on your own a long way from home and someone wants to kill you or, maybe worse, take you hostage and cut bits off you. It's when you are the last man left standing and the bandits are coming for you, grinning through their beards.

As you work your way through the book, you will learn how to avoid being killed or captured when things go wrong, escape if you are captured, steal food, steal transport, find your way home and fight to kill in the dirtiest ways you can imagine. Or maybe dirtier than that. This book is about survival in rough conditions: when you have been taken hostage or prisoner of war, when you have crawled out of a burning helicopter behind enemy lines and the enemy are coming or when your mates have all been killed in a fire-fight in bandit country – and the opposition are closing in on you.

I don't do 'politically correct' and some of what I teach here will shock any reasonable person. The fact is that war happens in a world different from your safe civilian life where you can call for Mummy or sue someone if you trip over your own feet. This is about the real world where power, as Robert Mugabe once said, flows from the barrel of a gun.

Perhaps the morality of killing and stealing to stay alive may offend some people who lead sheltered lives. But then they don't need to read this book. You do. So, if you are of a tender disposition, don't read on.

# Why Do You Need This Book?

What I have to say is mainly for soldiers, but if you are working as an undercover operative, in embassy or VIP protection, as aircrew overflying bandit country, or even going backpacking or exporting goods into some parts of the world, what you are doing might get you into some serious trouble and the tricks and tips explained here just might swing the balance your way long enough to keep you alive.

So, if you choose to travel to exotic locations, visit interesting people and either sell them stuff, steal their secrets, steal their oil or just shoot at them, one day something might go wrong and you could find yourself with a pressing need to escape the enemy and get home. That enemy might be a bunch of drugged-up kidnappers, crazy religionists or just the sworn enemies of your country. Best to know what you are doing if that happens, eh?

Depending on the situation, what you need to do to get home might be a brisk downhill walk to the highway. Or it might mean killing the people holding you hostage, breaking out of the safe-house, evading your pursuers, stealing food and transport, and meeting a submarine off the coast. Here I am going to tell you how all these are done. So you know what to do when it happens to you.

Someone once said that being a soldier was 99 per cent boredom and 1 per cent pure terror, and my only comment is that there may be a little more terror. The truth is that most of the time in the military you are eating, sleeping, getting drunk or waiting for something to happen – sometimes for weeks or months on end. Even special forces on sneaky missions are only in contact with the enemy for brief periods as a rule.

It is a strange feeling to be driving or flying or walking a patrol or eating in the mess hall with your mind on your girl or your dinner and suddenly have an explosion throw your transport about or knock the walls down. Then the situation kicks off with a bang, all hell breaks loose and people are dying left, right and centre.

If you are following your Standard Operating Procedure (SOP) properly, you have to be pretty unlucky to be killed in the first moments of an attack by bomb or gunfire. What happens in the following minutes is where most people fall short and where your actions – knowing what to do and doing it – can make the difference between living and dying. So living or dying is up to you really.

I have broken down the many ways you can come unstuck into five different scenarios. By looking at how to survive and escape each of these cock-ups in turn, we will cover most of the crappy situations you can find yourself in and give you a shovel to get yourself out.

I don't want you to think I have enough magic tricks to get you out of every possible scrape, but, if you remember what I tell you when you find yourself up to your neck in the sticky stuff, then just one of these tricks could mean the difference between coming home for some well-earned Rest & Recuperation and your poor old mum crying her eyes out.

There are no guarantees with this book. It is just designed to improve your chances, to put the odds a little more in your favour when the locals want their country back. The tricks I'm going to teach you might not work every time, and you certainly won't need them all, but one trick only has to work once *for you*. And that will make all the difference between watching a TV news report on some poor sod who got killed in some God-forsaken place and being him.

Knowing what you do for a living, could any of the following happen to you?

Could the aircraft you are travelling in come down in harsh or enemy territory?

Could your fighting patrol take such a hammering that you are left on your own behind enemy lines?

Could you be captured by the enemy and taken prisoner of war?

Could you be taken hostage by criminals or terrorists?

Could you find yourself hunted by a mob at home or abroad?

If you can answer 'yes' or 'maybe' to any of the above, this is the book for you.

Keep a copy in your back pack.

By now you're probably asking, who are you to tell me anything? I don't want you to think I am any sort of super-soldier. There are many, many men braver and more experienced than I am. If I have any talent it is for working things out and explaining them so anyone can understand. Of course, I have been around a bit and seen some action. The fact that I am still here to tell you about it means I am either very, very lucky or I know what to do when things get hairy.

The next bit is something of a life story but don't think I am showing off here. It's just that, if I don't tell you something about what I have done, why would you listen to anything else I say?

When I was 16 I joined the British Army as a boy soldier. I became a junior leader paratrooper, which means I was picked to be trained up to organise things. The problem was, I was a little bit crazy when I was younger and managed to get myself into all sorts of scrapes. I was fine with discipline but if anyone wanted to have a go with me I was game. I was once locked up for kneeling on a sergeant major's chest and trying to strangle him. In those days, boy service was different and 'locked up' meant standing to attention for 18 hours a day facing a locked door with a peephole. If you were seen to move, a large sergeant – in my case a fierce Scot – would come in and smack you.

After a year of intense training and having the rough edges knocked off me, I was sent to adult service with the Parachute Regiment. But first I had to do what is called P Company, even though I had already done it, including six weeks in the Welsh mountains as a boy soldier. P Company is the selection process by which the Paras weed out the tender souls from among those who want to become airborne warriors. Basically it involves lots of fitness training, weapons training and being screamed at, but there is also a series of quite long marches carrying weight to test determination, as well as the Trinasium, which tests nerve by requiring you to walk along scaffolding poles about 50 feet (15 metres) up and touch your toes, jump from pole to pole and so on.

One of the exercises, known as milling, involved going into a boxing ring with gloves on against someone of roughly similar size. You had to try to beat the hell out of each other for just a minute without turning away. It is surprising how tiring this can be even for fit young men. I was 17 the first time I went into the ring and was put up against a 29-year-old boxer who had just come out of military prison. He hit me until he couldn't hold his hands up and I was able to knock him down. It didn't matter who won, of course. The whole point was to ensure the recruits were not so frightened as to be unable to face someone in a boxing ring and keep facing them while taking some punishment. All boys should do this at school: it would stop bullying.

There were some interesting characters who joined the Paras. One of the recruits – I'll call him simply J – could make a crucifix by supporting his entire body weight on his fingertips with his arms outstretched between two lockers. He could also break a house brick with his fist in the palm of his other hand. An assault course is used to test stamina by making the runners break their stride to get over obstacles. J went round the three-mile Para assault course in record time and at the end his heart had not significantly increased its speed so a medic was called and he was rushed away in an ambulance. It turned out he had an oversize heart and big lungs.

In those days there used to be a fair amount of beating

of recruits by instructors, and this I support entirely as anyone too soft to handle it should not be there. Soldiers are paid to fight and kill and should not be so tender as to get teary-eyed at a few slaps from a non-commissioned officer. The instructors could see what an awkward sod I was and made my life absolute hell with extra duties, extra milling and plenty of beatings. At the end of the six-month course, which I passed, they told me I had missed the first day and would either have to leave the unit or do it again. So I did it again.

The next time round was no more pleasant, but I think the instructors were coming to think that I was such a nasty piece of work they would put up with me in their regiment. The whole idea of a Paratrooper, of course, is that you should be able to point them at a target and unleash them in the certain knowledge that they will either win or die trying.

Remember I said I was crazy? Well, after passing the third selection course I put in for a transfer to a tank regiment, the Royal Hussars. There I learned about armoured warfare in between tours of duty in Northern Ireland and some 'secret squirrel', or undercover, work.

At 19 I applied for the Special Air Service straight after a Northern Ireland tour. I am not a natural runner and much better suited to long marches, so the initial few days of selection almost killed me after four months spent sitting in a Land Rover or watchtower. When the SAS major in charge of selection asked me what I wanted to do, I said I would come back in six months.

My colonel in the Royal Hussars generously gave me six months off duties to get fit for the next SAS selection course. Every day for those six months I did three four-mile runs, two hours' swimming, two hours' boxing and two hours' circuit training and finished with a 12-mile run carrying a 75lb track link from a Chieftain tank. At the end of the 12-milers I always sprinted the last quarter-mile and got my pulse up to 200 beats per minute (bpm). When I was properly fit it came back down to 54 bpm in five minutes.

To cut a long story short, I went on the next selection course and passed comfortably. The greater part of SAS selection is a test of determination by daily long marches carrying weight. For me the hardest part was the timed runs at the beginning, in which I managed to come last – out of 105, I think it was. But only half a dozen passed the entire course. Having got through selection I then smashed myself up – bust my skull and hip – coming off a motorbike going home for the weekend. After five weeks I was back at Hereford with Demo Troop and stayed there for the best part of a year before moving on to work with another unit. Let me say for the record, so there is no misunderstanding, that I never went on active service with the SAS nor CRW nor ITU nor MI5.

I left the British Army to go to Zimbabwe – Rhodesia as it was then – and fight in the Bush War for Ian Smith against Robert Mugabe. Not only was Mugabe a terrorist but he was also a supporter of the communists, who were the biggest threat to the Western world in those days. From a youngster I have been totally against communism as I believe it destroys everything good in humanity – motivation, self-respect and self-responsibility for a start.

Right or wrong, I have always done what I thought right, so off I went and had a great time. Full-time warfare in a warm climate suited me and I got on quite well with the other characters there. I have the Parachute Regiment instructors to thank for knocking the rough edges off me and allowing all this to happen. Thanks, guys.

Although initially I was sent to the Rhodesian SAS – properly called C (Rhodesia) Squadron 22 Special Air Service Regiment from colonial days – it was by this time made up of ultra-fit youngsters rather than seasoned soldiers and was a totally different organisation from the British SAS. Owing to my having experience with armoured vehicles and the Rhodies getting some shiny new ones from South Africa, I ended up in the Rhodesian Armoured Car Regiment with a bunch of interesting guys and misfits, including some ex-French Foreign Legionnaires, a bass player from Louisiana, an early computer geek and a Yank stunt driver.

Our armoured cars, Elands, were far too valuable to risk on the mined roads so most of the time we operated as infantry. An Eland was a four-wheel-drive vehicle powered by a tiny, high-revving 2.2-litre petrol engine and mounted with a 90mm medium-velocity main gun. It had a coaxial .30-inch Browning machine gun, which means it pointed the same way as the main gun, and a similar Browning mounted on the top of the turret. Elands are surprisingly good across country and work well in the bush. The trouble was that they were as vulnerable as anything else to a mine on the road, so we infantry had to walk in front when they went out. That really puts your self-esteem in its place.

In the last year of the war we were out in the bush for perhaps all but a month and during that time in action almost every day. There is no way we could catch the super-fit African guerrillas, so we let them know where we were dug in and got them to come to us. All you had to do was give the locals a can of corned beef to dig a trench and straight away they would tell the opposition where you were. This saved a lot of footwork but always meant you would be outnumbered by more than ten to one.

After a while I ended up in charge of my own little team, over 180 men at one point, and fought all over Rhodesia and into Zambia and Mozambique. I got myself blown up a couple of times and collected 13 pieces of a Russian hand grenade. For more war stories, you need to read one of my other books, as I'm not repeating myself here.

When the Bush War finished in 1979 I tooled around Europe and then went over to join the South African forces with my good mate Yves Debay, who has since become a famous war correspondent and author owing to being able to write better than what I can. In French anyway.

In South Africa I started out as an instructor with the country's special forces – the Reconnaissance Commandos – then got involved in all sort of things which sound a lot more glamorous now, written down, than they seemed at the time. I was pulled in by BOSS, the state secret service, to work against a mercenary operation, I was contracted to recover stolen diamonds from runaway diamond dealers, teach unarmed combat, look after VIPs and all sorts of things like that.

I still like to keep my hand in by staying in touch with what is happening and a little consultancy work.

But I don't know everything. No one does. So, while you are reading this book, remember that what I say is as much to make you think as to be a rule book. Think about what I tell you and use what serves or do something cleverer and tell me about it. To give you an idea of what I can teach you, in a little while I am going to show you how to take a handgun off your captor. It might only work two times out of three but that is better odds than the certainty of being shot like a dog while a hostage – or much worse. It has worked for me twice in a row, so I am trying not to get into that situation again as I feel like I have used up my luck.

I'm not going to tell you which bugs and weeds to eat as I don't eat bugs. I eat meat when I can get it and vegetables when I have to. And I'm not going to tell you how to make an environmentally friendly wigwam either. If you have time to make a fancy shelter, you aren't moving fast enough.

But I am going to show you how to escape from disaster or the enemy, how to avoid recapture by tackling anyone who gets in your way, how to survive in enemy territory and how to make your way home. To do this you are going to have to learn how to deal with hostage-takers, escape from a prison cell, evade pursuit, steal food, steal transport, confront the enemy or anyone in your way and travel fast and light.

There are no prizes for making staying alive hard work. So if you want to learn about picking berries and mushrooms you have the wrong book in your hand. But I think I am the only guy ever to have put on weight during an SAS escape and evasion exercise.

As for where you could get yourself into trouble, it could be just about anywhere outside North America or Western Europe. The main places you will serve as a soldier at the time I am writing this are Iraq and Afghanistan. Clearly the locals in Iraq don't wish you well and Afghanistan will still be a trouble spot when we are long gone.

When the Russians were trying to hold down Afghanistan, the CIA were making things difficult for them by supporting the very people they and we are fighting there now. There is probably a moral in there somewhere. Anyway a mate of mine was contracted by the CIA to deliver a load of Stinger anti-aircraft missiles to the Taliban so they could shoot down the Russian choppers. He managed this by carrying them over the Pakistan border on camel-back. For some reason, afterwards, he decided to become a flower seller – perhaps because he is of Dutch descent – and when I last heard he was set up in Colchester, England, selling flowers by the truckload.

The Soviet empire has broken up officially over the past 20 years and so it is fraying around the edges as nationalists vie for power in the breakaway states and the Americans and others try to get what they want too – usually oil and/or minerals. This always leads to minor conflicts and businessmen are always either spying or accused of spying, which amounts to the same thing from your perspective as a soldier or other involved party.

The Balkans are still a little hairy and something may kick off there any time but the likely candidates for your services are South America, where everyone wants the oil and commodities, Africa for the same and the Middle East just for the oil. Something may kick off around the edges of the new Russian empire shortly too.

Of course, you could be held hostage by terrorists in

the UK, mainland Europe or the USA, and there is always the chance you could you find yourself facing a breakdown of society and civil unrest owing to a political or environmental disaster. Earthquakes and floods seem to be getting more popular lately.

# How the Book
# is Laid Out

There are countless ways that things can go wrong for you in a combat situation. What I have done is pick a few situations which cover most of the possibilities and show you how to get out of them. Then, when something serious does go wrong for you, the chances are that you can mix and match the ideas and procedures I have talked about and use them to cover your arse.

Each of the situations starts with something going wrong. Sometimes they wouldn't have gone wrong if someone was doing their job correctly and sometimes these things are just bad luck. Whoever was to blame, there is no point whining when the bullets start flying. Much better to know a plan so well that you operate as if on autopilot.

So, in Part One, we are going to look at your chopper being shot down, your patrol being hammered, your being taken a prisoner of war, being taken hostage and finally being confronted by a screaming mob. In each case the first step is survival at the scene of the incident followed by breaking contact with the enemy, but I have given a separate chapter to each of these scenarios.

The next stage, covered in Part Two, is keeping out of the enemy's hands while moving across country. This means dodging searchers, stealing transport and dealing with anyone who gets in your way. Anyone who sees you is likely to inform the opposition and must be eliminated as they cannot be taken prisoner. These procedures are similar to whatever happened before, so they are covered just once.

Part Three deals with the last stage: keeping yourself alive while travelling. This means patching yourself up if you're hurt, stealing food and water, making shelters if appropriate and navigating your way home.

At the end of the book there is a series of checklists so you can see at a glance what you might need to take with you in a variety of hazardous situations.

Now let's get to it.

**Part One**

# How To Break Contact With The Enemy

These first five chapters each cover one type of disaster in detail. What they all have in common is that something has gone wrong for you and the baddies are calling the shots. This means you need to stay alive through the initial encounter and then break contact with whoever the bad guys are. That is what it comes down to in each situation, although each requires a different set of tricks, as you'll see.

# Chapter 1

# Escape When Your Chopper Is Shot Down

Because of the way modern warfare works, with its high mobility and usually lots of ground to cover, choppers are the taxi of choice. They can not only put you down on a dime on any sort of ground so you don't get spread out or lost, but can also pick you up from pretty much anywhere and take you home again when you have done what you came to do. Generals love them.

First of all, we are going to look at helicopters making sudden, bumpy landings, because as a combat soldier you will be riding around in one every other day and I want to give you that warm, secure feeling we all love. The thing is, sometimes choppers do get shot down and sometimes they come down among people who are not our friends. This chapter is all about what you do then.

## WHY DO WE USE HELICOPTERS SO MUCH?

In the tactical arsenal of a modern army, helicopters play a vital role in moving troops relatively short distances quickly so as to achieve localised superiority of firepower.

If you have read any tactics at all, from the British Army Staff College training manuals to *The Art of War*, written around 600 BC by the Chinese general Sun Tzu, you will remember that the first rule of winning any engagement from section level to whole armies is concentration of firepower. By obtaining a localised superiority of firepower, be it rifles, longbows or half-bricks, you will defeat the enemy in that place and have troops left over to fight elsewhere. Repeat this and you will win any conflict. Simple stuff, war, isn't it?

So, if you are trying to kill or neutralise insurgents in a huge country with a handful of troops, you use choppers to move your small numbers of troops around like chess pieces and concentrate them on even smaller numbers of the opposition, however numerous they are in total, and beat them in that place at that time. Obviously this takes lots of organisation and lots of choppers. And while they are moving you around, the opposition are going to shoot at you, aren't they?

## WHAT ARE HELICOPTERS' WEAK POINTS?

Choppers are not totally invulnerable, whatever the training manuals say, so let's look at their two main weaknesses. First, they are relatively slow compared with fixed-wing aircraft and, second, they have to fly low a great deal owing to the jobs they do: much of the time they are landing and taking off in bandit country.

Choppers fly slowly because of something called retreating-blade stall. Miss out this paragraph and the next if your eyes glaze over at technical spec. I put it in because I know some of you love it and use it to chat up the girls. All rotorcraft, that is helicopters and autogiros, are physically limited to a top speed of around 200 knots (230mph/370kmph) whatever engines you put in them, because as they move forward through the air one side of the main rotor is moving forward, advancing, while the other is moving backwards, retreating, relative to the direction of the aircraft. The advancing blade always moves through the air at its speed of rotation faster than the aircraft's speed. The retreating blade, however, always moves through the air at its speed of rotation slower than the aircraft's speed. As the aircraft flies faster there comes a point where the retreating blade is not moving through the air fast enough to support that side of the aircraft and the aircraft flips over. Bet you never thought about that, did you?

To reduce this problem, in the rotor head there is a sort of gearbox which alters the angle of the blades as they turn, flattening the angle of attack on the advancing blade so it doesn't generate too much lift, and steepening the angle of the retreating blade so it generates as much lift as possible. But there is a limit to how much lift can be generated on the retreating side, however steep the angle of attack, so eventually, when the aircraft reaches a certain forward speed, and the retreating blade is moving slowly enough relative to the stationary air it is flying through, there is not sufficient lift to hold up the aircraft and it rolls over. In a technical sense, this is a really, really bad thing, so the air speed is restricted to what the main rotors can handle. In practice, most helicopters are limited to an air speed of around 207 knots (180mph/290kmph).

Helicopters spend a lot of time landing and taking off in places where they are not welcome and therefore they are open to receiving fire. There is little that can be done about this other than making them tough when you build them, and for the commander, at the operational planning stage, to use top cover (fixed- or rotary-wing ground-attack aircraft), darkness or dead ground to protect a helicopter when he can.

## WHAT ARE HELICOPTERS' STRONG POINTS?

The good news is that choppers are a great deal tougher than they look. I will say right away that I have never been in a helicopter crash of any kind, although once a Hercules I was travelling in out of Belfast Airport had an engine go up in flames and we had to transfer to another. I have, however, been in countless helicopters older and frailer than anything you will fly in and they have been well shot up by ground fire without catching so much as a cold.

A few years ago a chap who owed me a favour gave me a ticket to the VIP tent at the UK's Badminton Horse Trials. This is where lots of pretty girls in tight trousers and cute jackets ride around a sort of obstacle course for horses in the grounds of a big country house. And lots of toffs come to watch them.

Now my wife is very keen on horses, so off we went. She took herself to where they watch the horses and I settled down in the tent with the free booze. I will talk to anybody for a beer and I spent the entire day getting ratted with a man from a helicopter manufacturing company. I know for a fact I didn't see a horse all day but I did see a lot of inside stuff about the latest military choppers as the guy, who obviously thought I was someone else, tried to sell me a fleet of them. This was the sponsor's tent, after all, so there were promotional videos and glossy magazines and all sorts. Laugh? I nearly got the beer in.

When the bar finally closed we came out to see the rain had been coming down in buckets all day and the car park, essentially just a field, was a muddy swamp covered in millions of pounds' worth of late-model motors sunk to the axles and all waiting for a tractor. I don't care what you paid for your 4x4 – if it doesn't have the right tyres on, it will not get you out of the mud. Earlier the same day my wife had expressed her displeasure at our turning up in my old canvas-top Land Rover with mud tyres fitted, rather than in a smart saloon, but it was one of the few vehicles that got out of the field under its own steam so that probably proves something. To add insult to injury, my wife had to drive the beast home as I was in no fit state.

The point of this story is that, straight from the horse's mouth, so to speak, I was convinced by this chap with his films and design spec that even an economy-model Westland chopper wouldn't feel anything less than a .50-calibre round anywhere on the airframe and that the blades were so tough that if they hovered down on to a telegraph pole they would slice off the top without harming the machine! This little test has been filmed, which makes me wonder who they got to fly the thing.

Modern military choppers are even tougher, with high-spec armour not only around the crew, engines and fuel, as you might expect, but also under the floor where the passengers sit. This can be a very comforting thought when small-arms fire is pinging off the tin or whatever the body-shell is made of. Certainly there is no way anyone can spoil your day with a peashooter.

When you next fly in a chopper and some sod is shooting at you from the ground and the bullets are bouncing off the armour, just remember me flying in the old American Hueys with the pilot sat in a seat beaten out of ¼-inch steel plate and us grunts lying in the back on pieces of rubber conveyor belts. Happy days.

Anyway, the higher up you are in the air, the harder it is to shoot you down, whatever you are flying in, because bullets, even from an HMG, or heavy machine gun, run out of steam very quickly as they climb against gravity rather than travelling flat and roughly parallel to the ground. Rockets use a lot of fuel, as anyone who has watched a spacecraft launch will know, so every type of rocket or missile is limited, by the amount of fuel it can carry, as to the height at which it can shoot something down from. More fuel means a bigger missile is needed to carry the fuel and then using more fuel to lift that fuel, so you have a vicious circle. In short, it takes a far bigger missile just to go a little higher. That's why space rockets are so big.

Oddly enough, from the way they look to my eye, choppers can fly pretty high. So as not to give figures for anything useful to the opposition, I have to be vague here, but given the chance choppers can fly way over what a hand-portable missile can reach. So you are safe when cruising at altitude.

The problems come when you are contouring, following the valleys to keep under radar, looking for something on the ground, landing or taking off.

## WHICH WEAPONS THREATEN HELICOPTERS?

So what do the opposition have that might hurt you? I suppose it depends on who the opposition are and, since the purpose of this book is to cover most of the options, they could be anybody. In principle, a government defending its land or an army holding part of a country is going to have much larger reserves of cash and equipment than the alternative: a guerrilla or terrorist force who are effectively in hiding among the population on land you control – sort of.

If you are up against an army holding ground, they will have effective anti-aircraft weapons, which are generally missiles controlled by radar but might be high-tech guns controlled by radar. You can't fool guns and eyeballs but sometimes you can fool missiles with tin foil and so on to mislead their targeting systems. Choppers will not be used for ferrying troops around until this threat is neutralised by ground-attack fixed-wing aircraft or helicopter gunships. The way they generally do this is... Well, let me tell you how the weapons work and then you will see how they are defeated.

The most effective type of anti-aircraft system is a battery of guns or missiles covering an area – say a city or a battle-group – and linked together by long-range radar and a fire-control system. Radar sends out a beam which bounces off approaching targets and is very effective at spotting anything which reflects the beam. In practice, that is everything except stealth aircraft – so you can see why these were developed.

Each missile launcher or gun in the battery, of course, has its own arc of fire, meaning the area that it has to cover. The radar-linked system picks up the threat at a comfortable distance and warns the appropriate weapons in the battery to find the approaching aircraft on their own narrow-band radars, infrared or whatever guidance system they have. Then, all things being equal, they shoot it down.

When a defender has this type of defence it is highly effective against most aircraft within its range until neutralised so in the Gulf Wars the first job was to send in stealth aircraft to attack the long-range radar and fire-control systems. These aircraft are equipped with electronics which pick up the defending radar and send their missiles back along the beam, so to speak.

With the actual radars out of action, the aircraft then go for the local radar sets, missile launchers and guns themselves. They are a slightly harder target, but we have kit which does all sorts of clever stuff to pick them out. We don't want everyone to know exactly how this works, do we?

For those of you interested in this sort of thing, I will now give you a few notes on a couple of popular, man-portable, medium-range, anti-aircraft missiles. Everyone else should skip the next two paragraphs.

A missile you want to watch out for is the RBS 70 and its variants. It is made by the good old Swedes and fires from a little stand which a couple of men can lug about. The good book says three. I hope you don't get them pointed against you in theatre as they generate a laser beam which the operator holds on to the target – you – so they cannot be jammed by electronic countermeasures or misled by flares. The missile is armed with a 1.1kg (2?lb) fragmented warhead fitted with a Saab Bofors laser proximity fuse and an impact fuse. They have been sold to Iran and Pakistan, so let's hope they keep the good stuff for themselves.

Our Russian friends, on the other hand, produced and deployed in 1983 a little beauty called Missile 9M39.

Part of the portable anti-aircraft missile system Igla (9K38), this is designed to defeat visually observed jet, turbo-prop and piston-engined aircraft and helicopters flying head-on and tail-on courses. This despite any amount of jamming or false heat signals. The missile is fired by a gunner from the shoulder in a standing or kneeling position and the launcher looks something like an RPG7 but with a much longer missile. The Igla has automatic generation of elevation and lead angles and a deep destruction warhead, and uses detonating fuel like an RPG in its propulsion system and a displacement circuit in a homing head which ensures the missile hits the most vulnerable components of the target, so allowing it to defeat modern aircraft and helicopters. It can engage a target at a range of 5,200 metres (17,100 feet) and a height of 3,500 metres (11,500 feet).

The sort of enemy you are likely to be flying over is a guerrilla or terrorist force which does not have the strength or technology to hold land against you. Or, if they ever did, they will have had the crap beaten out of them before you get there by our flyboys. See above.

So they are not going to have radar-controlled weapons of any kind. If they did our people would pick up their radar signal and plaster them before the sets were even warm. Let's face it, if they even switch on a mobile phone out in the sticks we have them in minutes, so they are limited in the technology they can use and they have to be clever.

What they do have is old, short-range but reliable weapons and a wish to die for the God of their choice. This means that they are often willing to shoot at you from a position where, after their one shot, they will probably meet their maker at the hands of our air cover. This makes them dangerous because threats don't work against someone who is willing and ready to die.

Their weapons, in principle, range from the Russian equivalent of the .50-calibre Browning heavy machine gun up through some heavier-gauge machine guns, through the trusty RPG7 or 9, to the occasional shoulder-launched guided missile like the Stinger. Tech-speak warning: skip the next four paragraphs if you prefer.

The FIM-92 Stinger is a personal portable infrared homing surface-to-air missile developed in the United States. It entered service in 1981 and is roughly on a par with the Russian Igla. The basic Stinger missile to date has been responsible for 270 confirmed kills of aircraft, but do be aware that this is the figure for those aircraft the Americans can admit to and there have been hundreds of others which they cannot – such as most of the Russian choppers shot down in Afghanistan.

The Stinger is manufactured by Raytheon Missile Systems and also under licence by EADS in Germany. Raytheon designates the missile as a MANPADS (Man-Portable Air-Defense System). It is used by the military of 29 other countries besides America. Allegedly, around 70,000 missiles have been produced.

Light to carry – if someone else is carrying it – and relatively easy to operate if you can manage a mobile phone, the FIM-92 Stinger is a passive surface-to-air missile, shoulder-fired by a single operator, although officially it requires two. The FIM-92B, an improved model, can attack aircraft at a range of up to 4,800 metres (15,700 feet) and at altitudes between 180 and 3,800 metres (600 and 12,500 feet).

Stingers can also be fired from the M-1097 Avenger vehicle – which is actually a US military Humvee 4x4 with a Stinger rack, a turret mounted on the back of the vehicle carrying two pods of four missiles – and the M6 Linebacker, an air-defence variant of the M2 Bradley Infantry Fighting Vehicle, which is tracked, amphibious and weighs about 27 tonnes (30 tons). A helicopter-launched version exists called the ATAS, or Air-to-Air Stinger.

The missile itself is 1.52 metres (5 feet) long and 70mm (2? inches) in diameter, with 10cm (4 inches) fins. It weighs 10.1kg (22?lb), while the missile with launcher weighs approximately 15.2kg (33?lb). The Stinger is launched by a small ejection motor that pushes it a safe distance from the operator before engaging the main solid-fuel two-stage motor, which accelerates it to a maximum speed of Mach 2.2 (750mps). The warhead is a 3kg (6?lb) penetrating, hit-to-kill type with an impact fuse and a self-destruct timer.

I mention the Stinger because, as I said earlier, when the Soviets were occupying Afghanistan, the CIA were shipping Stingers in for the Taliban to use against the Russian choppers and that is why they lost so many. Fortunately, there are few left in Afghanistan, but who knows where else they may be available or who might supply them to whom? If the opposition has Stingers or similar, they *will* shoot down helicopters.

The overwhelming majority of the time, there will be no Stingers or similar in theatre and all you will have to worry about are heavy machine guns and RPG7s or 9s. And these can only touch you when you are either on or close to the ground. The thing is, helicopters do have to land and take off and they use a lot of fuel getting up high, so they only do so when they have to. On top of this, tactical considerations, such as looking for roads and buildings or troops on the ground, mean that you will spend a large part of many flights within the range of the weapons which are available.

Heavy machine guns are not too much of a problem because, although they are in plentiful supply among the sort of terrorist and Third World nuts you are going to come up against, they actually don't shoot them very well. Really? Doubtless you think I'm spinning you a line. Listen to this: the lightest and most common heavy machine guns which will be a danger when shooting at you are the Russian 12.7mm DShK heavy machine gun and the Chinese W85 heavy machine gun, both of which are equivalents of the .50 Browning, with which you will be familiar. Like the Kalashnikov AK47, both are made so that they will fire even after being dunked in mud and not cleaned or serviced.

All in all, they are fine weapons but they are made to be fired from an armoured vehicle or static mount where the heavy recoil could be soaked up. They were not made to be fired from a homemade stand on the back of a pickup truck which lets them bounce all over the place while firing and hose their bullets everywhere. There is also the Vladimirov KPV-14.5 heavy machine gun, a bit of a monster, to which the same principle applies even more forcefully.

So when the opposition fire their machine guns at you they spray bullets in your general direction and the rate of fire, in the region of 350–600 rounds per minute, is so unlikely to hit you it is not worth worrying about unless you are caught on the ground. You would have to be very unlucky – and if you are that unlucky you could step under a bus.

What is a problem to choppers is the RPG7 or its later model, the RPG9. I won't go too much into the spec as you are bound to be familiar with this extremely popular Russian anti-tank rocket launcher. It is a 1.2-metre (4-foot) tube which sits on the shoulder and fires a sort of rocket. The rocket itself is made of two parts, a warhead like two cones stuck wide ends together and the propellant, like a long, thick candle fixed to the back of the warhead. The propellant slides into the tube and is ignited by a trigger which works some electric mojo and all the propellant burns in a split second inside the tube, blowing the warhead forward at a rate of knots. It always seemed strange to me that it was called a rocket because I always think of a rocket as something like a firework which keeps burning as it flies.

The warhead goes flying forward and when it hits something, or after 1,100 metres (3,600 feet), it explodes. The inside of the rear cone is plastered with explosive which, as those of you who have done the demolitions course will know, makes a shaped charge and focuses the blast forward. This blast, from this little rocket, will burn a 5cm (2-inch) wide hole through 28cm (11 inches) of armoured steel if it hits it reasonably square on. This is true. I have tested it in the same way as I tested the 66mm anti-tank rocket (LAW) because I didn't believe that either. I got hold of a piece of armour from an old aircraft carrier and put a few holes in it. Although the 66 is not as accurate as the RPG7, it is a great deal lighter, and both of them make lovely neat holes as if they were done with a milling machine and then a little molten metal was dribbled around the edges.

The blast works because the detonator in the front cone sets off the charge at exactly the right distance from the armour it is designed to penetrate. Of course, the RPG was made to make holes in the side of tanks and other armoured vehicles and fry whatever it found inside. The more common use of it to make holes in buildings works by the same principle and the timer or detonator kicking in makes it effective against troops in the open or when it hits the ground near a target without detonating. The reason you strap another skin of steel a foot away from the armoured surface of your vehicle is that the outer skin sets off the blast and the second stops the resulting unfocused blast penetrating the armour skin and frying you.

I once met a chap who had been riding in the back of a Unimog – one of those high-up off-road Mercedes trucks – when an RPG hit the tin-plate side and exploded. The focused blast cut his leg off below the hip quite cleanly and totally ruined his career as a tap dancer. He went on to teach armoured warfare and it always seemed to me there would be something demoralising for the students seeing him but, hey, how the military mind works.

More to the point, from our perspective here the detonator, or the timer if the distance is right, makes the RPG useful against choppers because, as sure as hell, a decent hit will bring one down. And RPGs don't get fooled by clever electronic gizmos. Another proof of the old saw 'Keep It Simple, Stupid'.

The way the RPG is used by the opposition against

choppers is the same technique as the designers intended should be used with the 66mm against tanks. A bunch of you get close and all fire at once. With a little luck, one shot should hit it just right and up she goes. Or down as the case may be.

So how does this work in practice? If you are in a chopper, the only time you are significantly at risk is when you are landing or taking off in a hot zone because an RPG rocket is too slow to hit a chopper flying high or fast. If they have any sense, the flyboys will plaster the ground with machine guns or napalm before they come down but sometimes they can't. And sometimes you want to be quiet.

In one well-aimed blow at a chopper, with a few dollars' worth of RPG7, the enemy can knock out a bunch of grunts, a highly trained crew and millions of dollars' worth of kit, besides scoring a huge propaganda victory and denting your side's morale. This makes choppers a much sought-after target. Because of this value, the bandits in some places pay huge rewards to anyone who brings down a chopper. Enough to buy four wives and a string of white camels besides making him the village hero.

Anyway, don't go all girly on me here: you have to use helicopters and they are rarely shot down. Perhaps a little less rarely than the generals would like you to believe, as some accidents are not as accidental as others, but all in all choppers are about the safest way to travel in a hot zone. Certainly they are my favourite form of transport. But if yours goes down and you are still alive and far from home you do need to know what to do. Before we look at what to do when you come down, let's see if we can stop them hitting you.

## IS THERE ANY WAY WE CAN DEFEND AGAINST THESE GUYS?

If you have the time and the support, there are a number of tactics you can employ to make life difficult for anyone having a go at a helicopter.

Chopper pilots are generally not suicidal, and definitely not stupid, which is why they are not grunts; so they fly high when there is a known risk in theatre and they land and take off as fast as they can. Some of the following is to let you know that you are not helpless in a chopper and some is to remind young officers.

If you have to contour along valleys to sneak under the radar or to keep your noise down until you drop on the enemy over a hill, fly as fast as you can and as low as you dare just to make a hard target.

Ideally, when choppers come in to the land they will be protected by gunships like the good old Apache or ground-attack aircraft like the Warthog. These will use thermal imaging and other kit to spot bandits on the ground, then use their cannon, rockets and bombs to wipe them out before you come within range. If you don't want the spec on the Apache or the Warthog, just miss out the next two sections.

The AH-64A/D Apache Attack Helicopter is designated AH-64D Longbow in its ground-attack role, when it is fitted with the Longbow radar as mentioned below. It is a twin-engined, single-rotor, army attack helicopter developed by McDonnell Douglas (now Boeing) and entered service with the US Army in 1984. It has been exported to Egypt, Greece, Israel, the Netherlands, Saudi Arabia, the United Arab Emirates and the UK. The USA has around 800 in service while over 1,000 have been exported to the rest of the world.

There was one upgrade in 2003, principally to the electronics that connect the Apache to the battlefield internet, and another is planned for 2011. The reason there have been no upgrades to the weapons systems is that, frankly, they are awesome.

The AH-64D Longbow Apache is equipped with the Northrop Grumman millimetre-wave Longbow radar. Externally this looks like a fat disc mounted on a short stem above the main rotor and allows the radar to peek over obstructions at targets while the chopper remains hidden from enemy fire. This Longbow fire-control radar incorporates an integrated radar frequency interferometer for passive location and identification of radar-emitting threats. An advantage of millimetre-wave radar is that it performs when visibility is poor and is less sensitive than longer wavelengths to ground clutter. The short wavelength also allows a very narrow beam width, which is resistant to countermeasures.

The Longbow Apache can effect an attack in 30 seconds. The radar dome is unmasked for a single radar scan and then remasked. The processors determine the location, speed and direction of travel of a maximum of 256 targets.

Under the stub-wings there are eight Hellfire guided missiles which are typically used against armour or field emplacements. In human-speak, these missiles can be individually locked on to different targets when the chopper just pops its radar dome up to see them, then they can be fired from below the enemy's horizon, which has something of an unfair feel to it. Full fire-and-forget mode is available as standard.

Beneath the nose is a roller cannon, the M230, which fires explosive 30mm shells at a rate of 625 per minute from a 1,200-round magazine. It can be locked on to a target by radar or made to follow the pilot's eyeballs. These shells will destroy even tanks from above.

The Apache can also be equipped with air-to-air missiles (Stinger, AIM-9 Sidewinder, Mistral and Sidearm) and the Advanced Precision Kill Weapon System (APKWS), formerly known as Hydra, family of guided and unguided 70mm rockets.

UK AH Mk 1 Apaches are fitted with BAE Systems' Helicopter Integrated Defensive Aids Suite (HIDAS), also chosen by Kuwait and Greece. HIDAS, which includes the Sky Guardian 2000 radar warning receiver, entered service on the AH Mk 1 in July 2003.

The Apache AH-64 was designed from its inception to be highly resistant to enemy fire and allow its crew to survive a relatively high-speed impact with the ground. Not only is the airframe tubing impervious to 23mm or smaller high-explosive and incendiary rounds, but also sheet armour made of boron carbide bonded to Kevlar protects the crew from direct fire and the explosion of fuel and ammunition on board. In addition, bulkheads separate the pilot and co-pilot, so that both cannot be taken out with the same round. In the case of a crash landing the crew seats are designed to absorb shock and the landing gear itself is designed to progressively deform and collapse to take the brunt of the impact.

The only thing anyone can reasonably say against the A-10 Thunderbolt (Warthog) Ground Attack Aircraft is that it is bloody ugly. Apart from that, it is the most efficient ground-attack fixed-wing aircraft ever built. It isn't ever so fast at a little over 640kmph (400mph) and it has a range of only 970km (600 miles) but it is thickly covered in armour, has two well-spaced engines and can fly on one.

It can carry 227kg (500lb) bombs or cluster bombs and can fire AGM-65A Maverick air-to-ground or AIM-9 Sidewinder air-to-air missiles. But what it does best is use its nose-mounted GAU-8/A Avenger seven-barrel Gatling gun. This fires high-explosive 30mm rounds at a rate of either 2,100 or 4,200 rounds per minute, meaning that as the Warthog cruises over it must feel like the fist of God coming down on you.

If you can't manage any air cover for whatever reason – shortage of time, assets or bright officers – you need to come in as far as possible from cover or likely firing position. An RPG self-destructs at 1,100 metres (3,600 feet) but a .50 machine gun will shoot through a brick wall at 2,000 metres (6,550 feet), so keep your eyes open. Speaking of which, anyone reading this who can ought to get their new recruits to see a .50 shooting through a wall as it encourages careful use of cover.

When you touch down, one chopper at a time, everyone should get out as fast as they can and spread out to make a ring around the chopper, all facing out. This way only one bird is at risk at a time and with each drop there are more men on the ground to defend the landing position. But you know all this, so just don't get lazy.

When leaving, just do as close to the reverse as possible – with the added bonus that you really ought to know who is around the landing area. On the down side, of course, it could be what we call a 'hard extraction', which is where the flyboys earn their pay and pick us up while we are all being shot to pieces. My thanks at this point to all the alcohol-pickled jocks who have done this for me.

If everything you can do to avoid being hit comes to nothing, or if the bloody thing breaks down and falls out of the sky, here's what you do.

## WHAT HAPPENS WHEN A HELICOPTER IS HIT BY FIRE?

After frightening you to death with the many ways and means a chopper can be shot down I want to give you some better news. When a chopper is hit by a man-portable missile, because the missile has such a small charge and the chopper usually has two engines, you are probably not going to die straight away and the chopper will probably limp home or freewheel down to the ground and land softly enough for you to walk away. Obviously, if both the engines give up the ghost of their own accord, you will also glide in.

From time to time you will also find yourself moved around by fixed-wing aircraft such as the good old Hercules but don't worry about that too much for the moment, as if a fixed-wing aircraft is shot down put your head between your knees and kiss your arse goodbye because you will almost certainly die. If you don't, follow the instructions for chopper crashes.

First of all, let's look at what happens when a chopper comes down. We will take for granted that you haven't gone up in a ball of flames. You might if you were hit by a big enough missile, but let's assume that didn't happen. Mostly, with choppers, you don't come down because the engines stop. Many choppers have two engines and can fly on one, which is good, but sometimes both are knocked out and sometimes they break down. I have never known a chopper go down with engine failure myself but they do sometimes have problems with the gearbox or the mechanisms which work the rotors. The more complicated a machine is the more likely it is to go wrong. I only trust an AK47 myself. KISS: Keep it Simple, Stupid.

So where are we? You were coming in to land with just one chopper for a covert insertion in bandit country and by sheer bad luck there happened to be a band of Taliban sat around behind a hut smoking dope. Half a dozen of them fired their RPGs at you all at once and one hit just between the engines.

What has happened to you is just about the most likely thing of all the bad things you could expect: a bullet from a heavy machine gun or shrapnel from an RPG has hit something vital in the airframe – not, of course, both of the pilots. If both pilots are dead, you are going to die too, so now would be a good time to pray to the God of your choice or send a quick text message.

Given that your chopper is coming down one way or another, the pilot will, if he has the two seconds it takes, switch to auto-rotate. This simply means changing the angle of the blades so they work like one of those seed things that spin down from trees or an autogiro. The blades act like a sort of wing for the chopper to glide down on. It will come down soft enough to walk away from, providing the feathering is started above a certain height. I don't think you need to know what that height is and there are some people we certainly don't want to know. It is enough that the pilot knows and he most certainly will.

There may be smoke and fumes filling the passenger compartment from electrical or fuel fire. The good news is that it may not be long till you touch down. The bad news is that it may not be long... I doubt there will be anyone with a gas mask handy but, depending on the transport, it may be possible to get a side door open without fanning any flames. The crew may be able to deal with this. Otherwise try to hold your breath.

If you happen to be over water, and I know this is quite unlikely but at the cost of a paragraph it could save someone's neck, then you need to remember two things. The first is that because the engines are high up the chopper *will* roll over and sink. This means you will have to follow the, hopefully, lighted signs or whatever underwater to the exit hatch. The other is that over water you really should have a life-jacket on but *do not* inflate it until you are out of the chopper or it will trap you inside at the highest point.

If you are coming down over water, there is an argument for bailing out before it hits but be very careful at night because it is almost impossible to judge the height. I don't know why but it is. As you might expect, I've done water drills in a chopper and it's thoroughly unpleasant. I don't like cold water at the best of times. A drop in bad whisky is quite enough.

If the machine is spinning, your tail rotor has been hit. It should stop as the auto-rotate takes effect but it may throw you around, so it is as well to be strapped in. If you are not spinning, you may be able to get an idea of the lie of the land by looking out of the window. I know this may not be the first thing on your mind but it is surprising how cool you can be when something does happen. Look for any markers like water features and mountains in the distance which may not be visible from ground level. This may give you an idea of which way to go when you hit the ground.

## WHAT DO YOU DO WHEN YOUR HELICOPTER HITS THE GROUND?

OK, so you are still alive. Your chopper hits the ground and the landing gear takes most of the bump. You probably have the best chance of escaping injury if you're strapped into your seat. Flat on your back works well sometimes but standing straight-legged is a definite no-no as this transmits the shock up your legs, as all Paras will know, and your hips will be injured, rendering you immobile and therefore probably dead if you've come down among unfriendly natives.

Remember, almost always there will be Friendlies close by, either top cover or men on the ground. Even if you are the only chopper in the area, your commanders will almost certainly know where you are and be sending help for Mummy's little boy. Just about the only times things get nasty are when there is a cock-up in sending a rescue party or you are on a 'deniable' mission somewhere you shouldn't officially be. Every other time you will only have to keep the bandits off for a very brief time – although it may seem longer.

Sometimes, however, you really are being dropped or picked up a long way from support. Very often in 'peacekeeping' operations, the bandits control most of the ground and your side are only going to be holding bases and towns. This means if you come down it may not be near help. The opposition may also be keeping the help tied up. On the other hand, you might be doing a job alone or as part of a small team and you might be dropped a long way from any Friendlies. In this case you might get shot down in the sticks – anywhere.

Here comes the interesting part: because someone has shot at you, you know for a fact that the shooters have seen you and almost certainly seen you coming down. If you are lucky you have come down out of their sight but you cannot really know this for sure and there may be other bandits in the area.

Nine times out of ten, you will have been hit landing or taking off and there will be other guys on the ground to help you out and keep off the opposition. If there were no other men on the ground, there will almost certainly have been other choppers to come in, put out a cordon, pick you up and take you away.

But this one went bad: no one was around to bail you out and hold off the bad guys, and just let's suppose for the sake of a nightmare that either the transponder in the chopper was put out of action so your friends back at base can't tell where you are, or you are working over the border in a country where you just shouldn't really be so they can't send in the cavalry after you. What do you do?

Your first imperative is to get yourself, your mates and your gear out of the machine before the fuel goes up. If you are being shot at, shoot back and try to get their heads down and spoil their aim. After that the first job is to patch up anyone who is bleeding heavily or failing to breathe on their own. You should know the drill: bleeding, breathing, heartbeat, etc. Stop your mates dying on you or their mothers will never forgive you. Then look to stop the bandits from finishing the job.

## BREAKING CONTACT

If you are being shot at, you need to break contact and get away. If there is no shooting going on, there soon will be if you don't get away from the crash site, so get a move on. Run if you can and drag your mates with you if they can't walk. Don't leave anyone behind unless you owe them money; anyone captured is going to be tortured and perhaps given a starring role in a video of the torture.

In the dark you will be harder to follow but also it will be harder to cover any reasonable distance. The trouble is, very soon there will be bad guys on the scene and they know that the crash site is where you started from, so it is not rocket science to follow you.

The best thing you can do to slow them down is to set up either an ambush or a few booby-traps along the path you are taking so that even if they have good trackers or can hear you go they won't follow you at the run.

If you are being slowed down a great deal by your wounded, pick a good runner to set up an ambush and leave him behind while you make your best speed. When the bandits reach him, he can nail a few of them and the rest will certainly slow down. As with all ambushes, he should only engage at absolute minimum range or there will be a shooting match rather than a killing and he may be outflanked and captured.

Timid ambushes are the best way to get men killed. I always try to let the opposition get within 6 metres (20 feet) or less before triggering Claymore mines or opening fire. This way you are sure to get some of them and the rest may find pressing business elsewhere. You may even get them all. At night use Claymores and grenades as they

**41**

don't give your position away. During daylight always make sure your weapon is dry-cleaned rather than oiled up as this will eliminate smoke and render you invisible. I wish.

The M18 Claymore, a directional fragmentation mine, is 21.5cm (8½ inches) long, 3.5cm (1⅜ inches) wide, 8.25cm (3¼ inches) high, and weighs 1.5kg (3½lb). The mine contains 700 steel spheres (10.5 grains) and a 0.7kg (1½lb) layer of composition C-4 explosive and is initiated by a No. 2 electric blasting cap. The M18 command-detonated mine may be employed with obstacles or on the approaches, forward edges, flanks and rear edges of protective minefields as close-in protection against a dismounted Infantry attack. (Claymore M18 technical specifications courtesy of FAS Military Analysis Network.)

A Claymore mine fires its load of 700 ball bearings mainly in an arc of 50 degrees to the front but the sides and rear are dangerous too, so you want to be more than 100 metres (320 feet) behind it when it goes off unless you are undercover. To the front, everything dies within 50 metres (160 feet), most things die within 100 metres (320 feet) and many things die up to 250 metres (820 feet) away. Think of a Claymore as the mother of all shotguns.

Claymores are set off by a wire and battery system. I love them with a passion because of their efficiency and the fact that I can be far away when they go off. But you do have to be careful setting them up. You do not want to be bending over a Claymore when it goes off. And there really is a danger of accidentally setting the mine off when arming it by triggering the detonator inside. The order of march for safe use is: discharge any static in the wire before attaching the detonator to the wire; and attach the wires to the detonator before putting the detonator in the mine.

Before attaching the wire to the detonator it is a good idea to twist both ends of the wire together for a moment to discharge any static which just may set off the detonator. If you are near to an exploding detonator the difference between one on its own and one in a Claymore is similar to that between being made to 'jump' and being turned into a body-bag-full of burger meat. Through the carelessness of not discharging the wire, I once set off a Claymore detonator – out of the mine, obviously – when setting up an ambush. It sent a little cold chill through me, so I only did it once. Be careful.

If you are making good time or don't have anyone competent to leave behind, set up a simple booby-trap every so often behind you. The easiest way to do this is with grenades and some cord. Tie or tape one grenade beside the track you are taking. A tree or rock is best but it can be on the ground. The higher it is the more people get a piece and the better the trick works. Loosen the pin by bending the legs together – if it is of the common split-pin type – so it comes out easily. Tie the cord to the ring on the pin and the other end to something on the other side of the track to make a trip-wire. Only this trip-wire, of course, doesn't trip anyone – it just makes them jump.

Don't underestimate grenades. In the old days the body of a grenade was made of a piece of cast iron weighing something over 0.5kg (1lb): egg-shaped in the case of the British Mills 36 and loo-roll-shaped in the case of the Russian equivalent. There was a 4.5-second detonator leading to a whole 28gm (1oz) of charge, which made quite a bang. The lump of iron was segmented to encourage it to break into small pieces and give everyone a fair share but the pieces were still relatively few and large. That's why the Mills 36 was called the 'Pineapple grenade'. But there was a chance you might not catch a piece – particularly if the grenade landed on flat ground and you could get on the ground too so as to miss the rising cone of blast.

Once in Mozambique we were storming a hill and the opposition were dropping Russian grenades on us. A big chunk hit a young American lieutenant in the backside and put him on the floor. I was trying to grind my way into the hillside belly-first but it was no good and a grenade landed a yard from my right shoulder. I just saw it land and started to turn my head away when it went off. Any sort of explosion feels like being kicked all over at the same time and taking shrapnel feels like the 'dead leg' where boys used to knee each other in the thigh to stop the muscle working for a while. Remember?

Anyway, I took 13 pieces down the right side from the sole of my left boot, which must have been crossed over my right leg, to my right eye ridge. Because I was close to the ground, and lucky, I was more pissed off than hurt, so I was able to return fire for a while with some success at a range of around 6–9 metres (20–30 feet). Then I tried to get out of the position and my rifle was shot out of my hand. Sounds more amusing now than it seemed at the time. One of the lads, a young Welshman called Davies, gave me some covering fire while I got out and we made it back to our base camp – in my case limping well. I still have the piece of Russian steel against the bone over my right eye but the point of this story is that, although the original purpose of a grenade was to stun the opposition and give you a chance to run up and bayonet them, they can certainly make people stop and think when used unsupported. Thanks, Taffy.

Modern grenades have segmented, brittle wire in them, so thousands of tiny pieces of shrapnel are produced and everyone within a few metres will certainly get some stuck in them. This will slow people down as it is very uncomfortable when it happens close up. Certainly the person who trips the cord will be dead or out of action and probably one or two men behind him if they are too close. This will almost certainly slow down the remainder. They may even feel it is their duty to wait for daylight or reinforcements.

Set a little trap like this every so often as you move away. If you are carrying wounded, delegate this task to a suitable man and give him enough grenades.

So what have you achieved here? You got down with minimum injuries because you were strapped in. You took a look out of the window, so you know the sea is behind those mountains a couple of days' march away. On the ground you got your injured mate out and patched him up so he will not bleed to death before he settles his mess bill. You knew the opposition were close and coming fast, so you moved away as quickly as you could from the crash scene and left a trail of booby-traps behind you to discourage rapid pursuit.

What do you do now? Well, if you just survived coming down in a chopper and got so far as to break contact, you need to do what it says in the chapters on staying free, feeding yourself and finding your way home. But, as you just don't know where you are going to come unstuck, maybe you ought to turn first to the next chapter.

## Chapter 2

# Escape When Your Patrol Has Taken A Hiding

**W**hat do you do when you are way out in bandit country and an ambush has killed all your mates? This chapter is for soldiers serving as infantry or special forces on the basis that you are going to have to do patrols of one sort or another; and when you are patrolling you are either looking for a fight or available to be ambushed.

If you are working somewhere like Afghanistan, you will know that the best our side can do is hold a few strategic points, river crossings, mountain passes, towns and so on. The rest of the place is bandit country. We may have the upper hand when we go out on patrol because we go out strong enough to take on anything we meet, and as a rule we have air cover, but, however you look at it, the opposition runs the countryside.

There is the ever-present chance of meeting a group of the opposition who are too strong for you or of being badly mauled by an ambush. The opposition are not fools and learn from our tactics, so they are going to try to hit you when you cannot call in air support. That generally means that when the weather is bad you are too far from base for a quick response or they already have your air assets tied up elsewhere.

In Iraq, at the time I am writing, we are holding just one or two key bases for political reasons. The opposition runs the show. So, if you are out on patrol in bandit country, you either win every contact with the enemy or you are deep in the shit.

There are lots of other places where democratic governments are fighting this type of asymmetric war by using infantry on the ground. Examples include eastern Turkey, where the Turks are up against Kurdish Muslim terrorists; Sri Lanka, where government forces have been facing, and beating, the Tamil Tigers, a Muslim terrorist group; and there is Chechnya, of course, where the Russian democratic forces are fighting Muslim terrorists.

Egypt has had problems in recent times with Muslim terrorists as its government has tried to develop the economy along democratic lines. In Lebanon Muslim terrorists attack neighbouring Israel, and any form of democracy they disagree with at home, while being safely supported financially by Saudi Arabia.

And there are several other places where democratic forces soon will be fighting terrorists. Ethiopia, being two-thirds Christian, is already having problems with a minority Muslim population and the Muslim terrorists they support.

Somalia uses its strategic position, with seaports at the mouth of the Strait of Hormuz and the Gulf of Aden, to launch pirate attacks against the world's commercial shipping coming through the Suez Canal. They actually hold Western oil tankers and other ships for ransom.

In the Indian subcontinent, Pakistan is backing Muslim terrorists against the Indian government in Kashmir under the pretence of seeking autonomy for that region.

It is not widely known because of news blackouts but there are areas of China where the central government is struggling to keep control of the local Muslim population.

There are some who think that there is Muslim money behind the resurgence of Irish Nationalist groups such as the Real IRA. It would certainly be a standard terrorist tactic to use Irish Nationalists as a proxy to weaken the British government. For sure, in the past the IRA has bought arms from questionable Muslim countries such as Libya.

Social unrest and more terrorism will begin with an angry Muslim protest against British resistance to the Muslim call for Sharia Law, other markers of a Muslim state or British foreign policy towards one or more foreign Muslim states. If I can carry a useful metaphor across belief systems, this is just singing from the same hymn sheet, for another favourite terrorist tactic is to make apparently reasonable demands which your supporters favour but which the government cannot agree to. In this case, Sharia Law for Muslims living in the UK, for example. This tactic gives legitimacy to the armed struggle in the eyes of supporters and the naive. Many non-Muslims do not know that all Muslims are obliged to support the spread of Islam by any means and to bring about Sharia Law where they reside.

If you are working with a special forces unit, things might be even more interesting, because you are somewhere like Iran or Pakistan, and you might find yourself the only survivor of the team, the opposition too close for comfort and no air cover or extraction because the operation is deniable. No one among the top brass or politicos wants to admit you are there or carry the can. And home is a long way away. If you don't get yourself out of the crap, they are going to claim you were lost and leave you to it.

The situation we are going to look at in this chapter is where you have come second in the fire-fight and you are pretty much the last man left standing. On your side at least: there are lots of men standing on the other side and they are laughing through their beards. So what are you going to do?

For the purposes of this exercise it doesn't matter if you were ambushed or just bit off more than you could chew when you were picking a fight. As I keep saying, the first thing is to break contact with the enemy. In simple terms that means getting out of sight and range of small arms. Next you need to slow down the pursuit – and pursuit there certainly will be. Then you need to call in an extraction if you have the means or you need to start the long trek home. This is where the survival bit comes in.

What I am going to show you here is how you survive the first encounter and break contact.

## PATROLS, FIELDCRAFT AND COMBAT SKILLS

You go out on patrol for one of several reasons: you might be doing a clearing patrol around your base to disarm the perimeter defences and count the bodies in the morning or you could be sitting in an observation position, hopefully hidden from the enemy, so you can watch what they are doing and call in an air strike. You could be on a special operations patrol going to blow up a bridge or meet an agent or you could be on what is amusingly referred to as a fighting patrol – as if there were any other sort – where you are actually going out looking for trouble: attacking someone's base, for example.

In practice, you might also be patrolling the local villages to show the flag and either give the locals confidence that they will be protected from the bad guys or, depending on who you are talking to, letting the locals know who is boss. All of these patrols are vulnerable to being ambushed or meeting up with the opposition on other than perfect terms.

With the increasing use of drones and satellite imaging there is coming to be less use of reconnaissance patrols and manning of observation positions. I am all for that, as sitting in a hide for weeks is a pain, but that just leaves you free to get into trouble somewhere else, doesn't it?

If you are doing your job properly by following the correct Standard Operating Procedures, you will generally avoid disasters. That is what SOPs are for. They usually include things like how much water, food and ammunition to carry, what level of medical equipment and so on. They also involve running through the main plan for the patrol and contingency plans for if the worst happens. Your patrol commander should brief you on all these variables.

All the men on the patrol should be proficient in their training as regards fieldcraft, be physically fit and as well rested as the situation will allow. Don't laugh, I know you have been working four hours on, four hours off for the last month. Fit men stay alert for longer under pressure and this gives a significant advantage.

Every difficult situation you are going to find yourself in when on patrol tends to be caused by the opposition creating a localised superiority of firepower, even if only for a brief period. Remember this concept, as it is what you have been trying to do all along. This means they ambush you and are all shooting at you from cover while you are in the open or you bump into a bunch of them and they call up reserves or help before you get your act together.

There are four points I am going to cover now which you should have been taught in your fieldcraft courses but I want to make sure you know them as they are really basic and important.

When you are on patrol make sure you keep your spacing, even if you stop or something interesting happens like someone finds something. Do not bunch up as this is how the enemy get you into a small enough area to kill all at once. While walking and spaced at intervals of around 5 metres (16 feet), your group will not get more than one man killed from stepping on the one mine, you will not all be killed by one mortar shell and you will be a lot more difficult to ambush as the whole group will cover much more ground.

Being spread out may mean some ambushes do not get sprung on you. They may let you go past as they are not sure of getting you all in the opening burst of fire. This is a good thing.

When you are moving into an area where an ambush is likely, such as a small valley or pass, send out scouts to move ahead and to the sides of the main body of men. This is hard work for them but they will come across the ambushers first, in their flank, and have you for support.

When you stop, be it for a smoke break or for the night, always make sure every man knows his arc of fire – the area he has to defend – and that these arcs overlap so that, if one man is lost, the arcs on either side of his place still overlap. This will make your position as strong as it can reasonably be, all things being equal.

YOUR ANTI-AMBUSH SCOUTS

YOUR MAIN PATROL

BAD GUYS

TRACK

When you are moving along a route, it should be split up into tactical bounds. The distance between these will depend on the terrain but they should not be more than an hour or two apart and be marked by a prominent object if possible. The idea is that if you get split up you return to the last point and regroup there.

When you are selecting a position to take a brew, sleep for the night or to hold for longer, always make sure it does not form a trap for you. There should be a choice of ways out so the enemy cannot easily hold you there and everyone in the patrol should know where these exit points are. A cave is generally a bad choice, for instance, but everything is a balance of benefits and drawbacks and perhaps the advantages of hiding or warmth outweigh the risks. Although you do have to wonder if the locals don't know about a handy cave: I would have it booby-trapped if I were them.

## WHAT YOU NEED TO BE SURE OF BEFORE GOING OUT ON PATROL

It should go without saying that everyone will have healthy feet and good footwear so they don't slow you down. Everyone's weapon should be clean and oiled or dry according to the conditions and the weapon. Oil is to sand what flypaper is to flies.

The patrol leader should always check the men's weapons and have them lay out vital equipment as men have been known to bluff in an attempt to hide loss of kit or avoid extra weight. I have caught men carrying balled newspaper in place of heavy equipment. They only did it once.

Preparing for a patrol is too late to teach basic soldiering skills and these should be drilled into the men well in advance.

Each mission is different, even if it is over the same ground. A good leader will brief his men in one group before each patrol to ensure everyone knows what his job is, how to call for backup, casevac (casualty evacuation), an air strike if appropriate, where the tactical bounds are, radio frequencies and a whole load of other bits and pieces according to the situation you are in.

From the British Army in the First World War there's a memorable word for patrol briefing: GSMEACS. I was taught this by an old sergeant when I was 13 years old and I still remember it, so you should too. You say it 'Gee-Smee-Acks' and it stands for:

Ground: What is the country like you are crossing?

Situation: Who is there and how friendly are they?

Mission: What are you going for?

Enemy: What enemy forces are expected in the area?

Atts. & Dets. (Attachments and Detachments): What extra personnel are attached and who is missing?

Command: What will be the signals for specific actions and events?

Signals: What are the code words and radio frequencies, etc?

When you are going to do something out of the ordinary like crossing a river or a barbed-wire obstacle, you should always try to have a rehearsal. Many men learn far better by being walked through something than being told or shown it written down. As these things can be a matter of life and death, it is worth the embarrassment.

## A QUIET PATROL

So everybody is in good shape and has what they need. Most people even know what is happening and you set off into the wilds. To get there you may hitch a lift in a chopper or be dropped off by taxi but sooner or later you and the boys are going to be on your own.

(If you are going on patrol in a town, if things kick off badly and you take a hiding, your reaction will be closer to dealing with a mob than losing a fire-fight, so see Chapter 5.)

Your commanding officer does not want you to disappear for a week and then come back to base smelling like a Turkish whorehouse. He would very rightly be suspicious of what you were up to and no doubt he would have been worrying about you. At the very least, he might have been dreading writing a letter to your mum.

To stop the old man worrying, you need to keep in touch with base while you are out on patrol. There may be an SOP to the effect that you check in each hour or at certain points in the march. Whatever, the idea is that your commander should know where you are and what is happening, if anything. This is pretty much a sitrep, or situation report. In it you will be passing back information which might be useful to intelligence before you get home and also you will be giving a progress report, so that, if the worst happens and you lose contact, the search party will know where to start.

I know you all have phones and tracing equipment nowadays but these things take time and trouble for your boss, so keep his workload down and let him know how you are getting on:

'Hello, Three Niner, this is Three One. Over.'

'Copy, Three Niner. Over.'

'Three One, sitrep at 14:23. Grid 12345678. Have reached point Glory. Am continuing. Over.'

'Three Niner, copy. Out.'

If you are on a special operation, and somewhere you really shouldn't be, then there may well be a radio blackout so the enemy cannot pick you up – unless you have the latest special communications equipment and if you have that you know what it does.

All the time you are out on patrol, it goes without saying that you are keeping your eyes open and watching for an attack. But more than this you also need to be thinking what you will do if you are attacked. Where is the nearest cover, where can you group your forces, where is the attack going to come from and where can you go to get away from the killing zone?

## WHAT SHOULD YOU DO IN NORMAL CONDITIONS WHEN THINGS GET WARM?

Everyone will know the SOP for a contact – or they will afterwards if they have been in just one. Being in your first contact, even if you don't get to shoot at anyone or even get hit yourself, does have a positive effect on you as soldier. Everyone is a little shaken up or over-excited the first time. The second time you will take it in your stride and you are a veteran.

When you come under fire, which is more than the odd round cracking as it goes past, you will return a burst of fire in the general direction of the bad guys and take cover as quickly as you can. Every situation is different but you will already have your eye on a good place close by because you have been picking them all along, haven't you?

Your commander on the ground will then assess the situation and send back a contact report. For some reason, this doesn't have a snappy abbreviation that I know of. Different armies with different radio procedures do it slightly differently but it is meant to tell your boss back at base that you have met with the enemy and what you are doing about it.

'Contact at 23:44 hours grid 12345678. Enemy in company strength. Am engaging. No casualties.'

So your boss wants to know when, where and who they are, plus what you are doing about it. You should tell him as soon as possible that contact has been made and then follow up with a report on how things are going if appropriate. You may have a different person to call on for air or artillery support if this is available.

Your unit commander's next action will depend either on his assessment of the situation or his instructions from above, but what it amounts to is that if he thinks he can win he will organise some kind of assault. Perhaps one team stays put to give covering fire and another moves out to the flank to assault the enemy. If the situation does not look so good, the options are more limited. The first option is to call in air or artillery support and let them give the opposition a good stonking with high explosive or napalm. Another choice is to withdraw to a better position to avoid the opposition's advance.

The trouble really starts when you are losing so many men that you cease to be a threat to the enemy and they begin to think of assaulting and overwhelming your position. Of course, if the contact begins with the bad guys ambushing you, you are off to a bad start already as ambush points are picked specially not to have any good cover close by and if there is any it should have been mined or booby-trapped. Sort of like paper, rock, scissors.

If the ambush was set up properly, you should have been killed in the first two seconds. This is why you avoid ambushes. Given that you were not killed, it was not done right. A proper ambush is set up so that it is sprung when the prey are within what is called a killing ground. A place where there is no cover and nowhere to go.

If there is cover you take it, but if there is none the only alternative is to charge the ambush. At least this way it gives you something to think about. This did once happen to me and we went straight at the enemy while another team gave us some covering fire from the flank and the enemy got up and ran. Our survival in this instance was pure luck and in no way due to skill or bravery. Don't count on being so lucky. If you are in an ambush and survive, you will try very hard not to be in another one.

If you come into contact with the enemy by choice, a fire-fight will take place, hopefully on more favourable terms. Traditionally the fire-fight continued until one side began to cause the other to get their heads down and realise the opposition was stronger. The stronger side would then follow this up with an assault on the position. But it has become common practice in recent years, if you are able and it seems the enemy is strong enough to make it worthwhile, to always call in an air strike and avoid the risk to your own men of assaulting the enemy on foot. That works for me.

## WHAT CAN POSSIBLY GO WRONG?

So, you have walked into a strong ambush but you are not dead yet because it was not set up right. You may take some comfort from the fact that ambushes are rarely set up properly. Alternatively, you have picked a fight with the local heavies. In either situation, you are heavily outnumbered, in a poor defensive position and taking casualties.

Things start to get intense when you can't win the fire-fight because you just can't get close to the enemy and they are calling all their friends to the party. This is where you start to lose the initiative and lose men. A numerous enemy will try to work their way around you so you cannot escape and when they are ready they will mount an assault with fixed bayonets and lots of screaming.

To avoid this, when you feel you are outnumbered and losing the plot, if you can you should pull your men back to keep them in one unit and prevent encirclement. This can be difficult to achieve and feels a very strange thing to do when the bullets are flying past your ears and your instincts say dig in.

As soon as you can, you try to call for air cover but you find it is tied up on another operation. Maybe the opposition are organised enough to mount a false attack on an allied base at the other end of the country. But suppose this time you get through and call for an air strike. When the choppers arrive, the opposition are well spread out and dug in. The choppers just cannot kill enough of them to make them give up.

Even worse, it might even be the case that the enemy have attacked you to draw the allied air assets such as Warthogs or Apaches close to their anti-aircraft missiles. That would be a real bummer, wouldn't it? So the choppers turn up and get shot out of the sky.

Probably worst of all is when you discover you cannot contact your base or anyone else. The opposition have radio-jamming equipment and you are starting to feel lonely because no one knows exactly where you are or even that you are in any trouble at all. No one is coming to help.

Scenario: you are on a mission in northern Iran to photograph and count trucks arriving at a secret nuclear factory. You bump into a patrol of the Revolutionary Guards and take some casualties. Our Government not only says you should not be there but also they will not send air to get you out or protect you.

The enemy are in force and your mates start dropping all around you.

You realise that you are losing the fire-fight.

You are on your own.

Most of your men are dead or wounded.

The remainder are struggling to maintain contact with each other.

## IF THERE IS ANYONE ELSE
## LEFT ALIVE, DO THIS

If there are still a few of you left alive and you are close together, you form a fire group for mutual support. To form a fire group, the group of soldiers should arrange themselves facing outwards, each defending an arc to the front and leaving no unguarded access to the position. In this case you should try to withdraw from the scene, employing the 'buddy system' you will be familiar with from training, although it is normally taught for use in the advance. Work in pairs, with one man moving while the other gives covering fire to keep the enemies' heads down or at least spoil their aim.

If there are several men left alive but you are

separated and unable to regroup at that location, you should each break away and, if possible, head to regroup at the end of the last tactical bound. As I said earlier, all professional soldiers will have split their route into segments called 'bounds' and marked by resting places or other markers to allow for this. Won't you? If you have just been attacked while on an ambush, the place to regroup is the rest area where you dropped all your packs and spare kit. There may be more ammunition and even men there. Failing this, get back to the end of the previous bound.

However, if you are the last man standing, you just need to break contact and put some space between you and the opposition. In a practical sense, this means break contact and run. When you are being overwhelmed it is difficult to create enough fire to keep the enemy's heads down, so you will probably be best to sneak away on your belly. When your position has been overrun, everybody there will be searched and the wounded may be either killed or saved to entertain the women. In several cultures the warriors give captives to their wives as they are more inventively cruel and may keep them alive for some days.

If you cannot get away you are better checking out with a grenade to the head. It is much the quickest and cleanest way.

Given that you are in reasonably fit condition you can try to make an escape. Drop any non-essentials and keep just your survival kit, water, a little food concentrate and your weapons. If you are lucky, it may be dark or night may be approaching and this will work in your favour for a while. Try to head undercover towards the last place your team stopped, the last bound or the waiting position for the ambush. Here you may meet anyone else who escaped and be able to pick up more stores and ammunition.

As you clear the area of the contact, try to set up at least one booby-trap, as shown in the previous chapter, as people will follow you and fireworks will slow them down. If your pursuers are Muslims, you have the added advantage that they are unlikely to use tracking dogs.

## DEALING WITH THE DEAD AND WOUNDED

Your priority is to keep yourself and your surviving mates alive. This means getting clear of the site and patching up anyone who is wounded. If you have time, however, consider the following as it is a service to your comrades: search the dead for personal papers and so on – anything which can identify your men or tie them to relatives or clubs etc. It is not very nice for the relatives to hear from their killers by letter or email and you don't want the terrorists making up stories about how unpleasantly Johnny died. And take the dog tags so your officers can do the paperwork properly.

The most difficult problem is dealing with the wounded. If you can move them, they will slow you down and may lead to everyone being captured and killed. I know what all the armchair heroes say on TV but this is the real world and it ain't pretty. If you cannot take the wounded with you, and that includes even someone with a relatively minor wound that is stopping them running, they will have to be left to be captured or kill themselves. It is better some survive than none at all. Even if it isn't very heroic, I think the survivors' wives and children would appreciate it.

## MEDICAL ISSUES

I take for granted that you were fit when you started – if not you deserve to die – but what you can do now depends on how badly you have been wounded. In a normal combat situation you just need to know enough to keep your mates alive until the chopper comes to casevac them back to a proper medic. This just means stopping severe bleeding, restarting the heart and keeping the breathing going for a few minutes. When you are out in the sticks without support, you may have to keep someone alive for days until expert help is available. Obviously some wounded are going to die but you can learn enough to do a lot of good. There is no excuse for anyone not being pretty handy as a medic. If you are not yet capable, get on the next medical course as it will come in handy.

See Chapter 12 for more on keeping casualties alive but for the moment you'll need a broad-spectrum antibiotic, as an injection or taken orally as appropriate. Make sure the wounded take the full course or they will not work. Anyone with broken bones or gunshot wounds is likely to be dead or left behind. If you manage to get them out, do what you can. Set the broken bones and splint them, cover the sucking wounds with plastic and seal them to keep the air out of the lung cavity and stop the lungs collapsing, sew up any large gashes and/or apply a pressure dressing to stop bleeding. For head injuries, just cover to keep the dirt out. You do not give morphine to head injuries.

Most wounds amounting to more than a shaving cut will go bad even in a cool, dry climate. To stop this you need to give out a broad-spectrum antibiotic and make sure the wounded take the full course or it will not work.

Assuming you have got away from the actual scene of the contact, what do you do next? You should have a very good idea where you are and the lie of the land if you have been on foot in the area, so that is not a problem. What is a problem is getting back to base without getting caught by the people who dislike you so strongly.

## Chapter Three

# Escape From A POW Camp Or Third World Prison

Now we are going to look at what happens when you are about to be taken prisoner of war by an actual organised body such as the army of a national government, or you are about to be arrested and held in a Third World government's prison for whatever reason. I'll cover how to escape from a hostage situation in the following chapter as this differs in significant ways.

You may have been ordered to surrender to a foreign army, you may have been wounded and captured, or you are being arrested by a police officer in a Third World country where you may or may not have been spying, trading illegally or whatever. You might not think so right now but these two situations have a lot in common, so I shall be dealing with them together here, though where the SOP is different I will point it out.

What becoming a prisoner of war and a prisoner of a state have in common is that both involve relatively professional organised systems for arresting people and keeping them captive. This means getting away from each situation has things in common too. Among other things, there are professional guards with less hatred for you than you might get with, say, terrorists. And they have rules, like not killing you, that they must more or less stick to. An important point is that the guards are there for a wage at the end of the month, not for the love of keeping you in a cell and tormenting you.

Another thing which state prisons and POW camps have in common is that they are both organised as a business rather than a one-off hostage situation. This means you will be one of many inmates and therefore may not be watched too closely.

Something which sets the two situations apart, however, is that in a POW camp soldier-prisoners will go to great lengths to help one another whereas the low-life in a prison full of criminals will steal from their fellow prisoners and inform on them for a smoke. I have been in both kinds and know well whereof I speak.

I was once checking out the weapons being tested by South Africa's special forces in Durban while I was serving with the South African Defence Force, as they called the army, and this involved moving some rifles to the docks for someone to take a look at them. Through a combination of unfortunate coincidences, someone saw a piece of a stripped rifle in a pack I used to train with and tipped off a certain Afrikaner officer who hated me with a passion. The Afrikaners used to refer to the English – and that means English visitors or English by descent – derogatively as *soutpiels*, meaning 'salt cocks'. To them the English, however many generations they spent in a foreign land, always kept links with the old country. So it was one foot in South Africa, one in England, and that other part of their anatomy in the sea between the two. Unlike the Afrikaners, of course, who cut all their ties when they left the Netherlands to live in South Africa in the 1700s to escape religious persecution.

There was a search of my room on camp – officially for dope – but really as a cover for a weapons search. There was a stripped-down weapon in my locker and this officer threw a wobbler, raving about spying and so on. Obviously no comms equipment, codes or records were found. But in short order I found myself in the local military prison, being at the time officially a South African soldier. There was no point in attempting to resist arrest as there was little they could do or prove – and I felt I would get some cover.

Anyway, the accommodation was spartan but comfortable enough, with a dozen young men sharing a room containing a dozen mattresses, but there was no nastiness. You often find that in military prisons the inmates are high-spirited young men who need bringing under control rather than villains who need gassing.

There was no interrogation for me, as they were concerned at that time about a diplomatic incident, so I just joined in with the other guys and kept my head down. I spoke some Afrikaans by this stage but most of the conversation was in English. We managed to get one of the guys' girlfriends to smuggle in 2-litre bottles of Coke which had been half-emptied and refilled with rum. One of the guys was some sort of kung-fu master who could hypnotise you just by looking you in the eye and twitching the muscles in his cheeks. He put everyone under and made us stick to the walls or mattresses or think our clothes were on fire. Great fun.

For something to do I organised a daily fitness training session to get us all out of the cell and into the exercise yard for a few press-ups.

As I have said, the guards in places like this don't generally have a problem with you so they will often cut you some slack for a quiet life. Booze and cigarettes work well to grease the path of life in any army. It was Christmas, so we even got the guards drunk and I ended up looking after an armful of Uzis for them. Sounds unlikely, I know, but I swear every word is true.

Anyway, the diplomats did their thing and in a couple of weeks I was made an offer I couldn't refuse: admit to being in unlawful possession of firearms and I would be given a dishonourable discharge from the South African Defence Force. What could I say?

Within a few weeks I was working on the door in the roughest part of town and making all sorts of new friends.

The first bit of advice I want to give you about being taken prisoner is: 'Don't be.' That probably sounds a real smart-arse comment until you hear what I have to say. How you are treated in any prison depends to a very great extent on where you are in the world. You ought to know where you are, so you should know what to expect when held. Given that you are going to be held, you can make a great deal of difference to your prospects of survival and escape by how you react to the situation.

## IT'S ALL ABOUT CHOICES

Once you hand over your gun you are powerless and the people who are holding you can do to you whatever they want. They can kill, beat, torture, starve, rape you and anything else they wish. Remember that. So, if you are being arrested by a state police officer in, say, Nigeria or Colombia, once you have decided against resistance and handed over any weapons you may have about your person, you are at his and his friends' mercy. Totally.

Knowing where you are, what you have done to get arrested, what they might find out about you later and what they might do about it are all things you need to take into account before you find yourself being held. You have to decide in advance if you are going to kill or disable the arresting officers to remain free, as if you want to stay out of prison this is by far the easiest time to do it. Once you are disarmed, stripped, beaten and in a cell it is a lot harder to get away. Of course, you may be killed trying to avoid arrest, so it's a trade-off between risks and benefits.

In a military situation, pretty much the same holds true. If you surrender to an organised state army, they are going to take you prisoner and put you in a cell. Who they are makes a great deal of difference as to what will happen next. If you are somewhere like Iran, they will want to make political capital out of you and, therefore, while they may interrogate or even torture you, they probably will not kill you. On the other hand, they may keep you prisoner for many years. If you were being held after some kind of border incident by a major power, you would probably be treated reasonably well and released within weeks, so it would not make sense to take the risk

71

of killing the arresting officer. You will, of course, have plenty of time to think about this sort of thing as you will know where you are operating.

In Durban I did a little job for a group of dealers in precious stones who were based in the city. It is the practice in that trade to lend stones to other traders on an honour system so they can show them to clients and hopefully sell them. In this case, another trader had tried to rip them off and skipped into Lesotho, an African mini-state entirely surrounded by South Africa and run by the locals. After a fashion. My task was to go in, find the guy and take the stones from him. With false papers, pistol and hired car, I went in and found the bank where he was based. This was perhaps not the most subtle approach as I was the only whitish face in the whole town but it did the trick and the stones were returned.

There are a couple of things I want to mention about this job which may be useful to you. The first is that when you park up in places like that a youngster will often come over and offer to look after your car. If you refuse you can imagine what you will come back to. When you do return you need to pay the little guy because if you don't a small riot will start and guess who will be arrested? You only need to give the kid a few coins and in many places this will feed his family for some time.

Which brings me to the police situation. This is just the sort of place where the police don't get paid for months on end and have to make a living with bribes, so when an officer comes over and asks for your papers be sure to place a few notes in your passport as this will get you a salute and you're on your way. Alternative responses will not.

I have never been in a position where surrendering to the enemy was a possibility. As a general rule you should not be surrendering to an enemy force unless you are sure you will be killed otherwise. And even then perhaps not.

## THE GOOD OLD DAYS

Being taken prisoner when the armies of Europe were fighting one another was quite a reasonable and honourable thing. If your generals had been outmanoeuvred and you were surrounded on the battlefield, and you had escaped a bayonet in the initial clash of arms, you were held in a prison camp until the end of hostilities. This went on from around the 1600s to the Second World War. There was even a humanitarian agreement between nations covering exchanges and treatment of prisoners, called the Geneva Convention, and Red Cross officials visited to maintain standards and deliver food parcels. Very civilised.

Fighting in the Far East was somewhat different. Japanese culture in particular held surrender to be pretty much the lowest thing a person could do and anyone who had surrendered was considered worse than a criminal as they were betraying their leaders and country; a person without honour or rights. A different culture and way of looking at the world.

Today we have a whole collection of potential enemies, none of whom is going to respect the Geneva Convention, either because they as nations don't think that way or because they are independent fighting groups who do not answer to any authority. Nevertheless, how you are treated if captured will depend entirely upon exactly who is holding you, what you were doing when captured and what you have been kept alive for. You ought to know this in advance and be able to use this knowledge to make your decision on how hard to avoid capture.

## HOW COULD YOU END UP A POW?

The very existence of a prisoner-of-war camp says that your country is fighting another organised state as otherwise you are effectively being held hostage by terrorists and I will cover that later as quite different principles apply. The only excuses for being a POW are these:

If you are wounded in action, even with a knock on the head or a flesh wound or broken leg, you may not be capable of resisting capture and will end up a prisoner. If this happens there is no choice but to hope you are lucky in your captors and try to get well enough to make a break later.

If you are an aviator and your aircraft is shot down, you may well be vastly outnumbered and captured as your parachute touches down. If your flyboy mates have been killing the locals, they are not going to treat you well. Some aviators are beaten to death on the spot. Clearly it is in your interest to do anything you can to avoid being caught and killed or carted off to a POW camp as it will not be fun and you may die of forced labour or torture. Flyboys are all trained in escape and evasion, so if you are reading this I suggest you get good at it.

If you are surrounded and absolutely unable to escape without certain death, you may consider surrender, bearing in mind what your treatment may involve. Better not to get into this situation in the first place.

A slightly different situation, perhaps, is if your whole unit has been ordered to surrender – this did happen in the past, for example in the Second World War when a whole British Army of 80,000 men was cut off and surrounded by the Japanese in Singapore. They were out of ammunition and food so their commander, General Arthur Percival, had no option but to order them to surrender or have his men slaughtered.

I have often thought about the pros and cons of surrender under orders and the conclusion I have come to is that a well-disciplined unit really ought to surrender, as the vastly outnumbered Royal Marines did on the Falklands. Of course, when the sneaky invasion was first launched, this was only a handful of marines against an army of Argentineans, and the marines did get their own back later, with interest.

In principle, the men should trust their officers to have made the correct decision in order to save the lives of ordinary soldiers. Some men will disobey orders, just like some of the marines did, and go on the run. Make your choice.

## HOW TO AVOID CAPTURE

If things have come to the stage where your position is overrun and your mates are dead, pretty soon you are likely to join them, so what I am going to explain here is a last-gasp effort to stay alive when the only available option is not to.

If there is somewhere to hide, take it. Under a vehicle or woodpile, just take what there is. The only alternative is this: cover yourself in blood if you can. Lie face down with a pistol in one hand under your body and a grenade in the other with the pin out. (Contrary to popular belief, you can remove the pin but the grenade won't detonate if you hold the lever in place.)

The correct way to check bodies on the battlefield is to approach them in pairs. One man stands off the head or feet pointing his rifle at the body while the other approaches at a right angle to search the body while giving his mate a clear shot. You should roll the body over towards you so that if it is lying on a grenade it will help protect you from the blast.

You want the opposite to happen if you're playing dead, of course, and it may well do as people are so careless. Listen for someone approaching, all the while praying that they come alone. As they come right up to you, roll over and shoot them in the centre of their body. If your wrist is cocked, watch out for the top slide of the pistol coming back and sticking in the top of your wrist as this is very sore. If they come in a group or groups, throw the grenade at the closest group and keep shooting.

The order in which you should shoot a group of people, if you have no grenade or some are still standing after the bang, is to first take the ones pointing weapons at you. Then take the ones who move as they have overcome the initial shock and may do something. Then take the others. Put only one round into each man as you will not have time to reload. You can finish them off later if time allows.

If there are less than half a dozen men close by, you stand a slim – but real – chance of survival. Make your choice.

There may be a chance to use smoke or further grenades, if you have them, to confuse the remainder, but this is a good time to put some distance between you and them. Get out of sight, then set the first booby-trap as explained earlier.

## WHY MIGHT THE POLICE WANT TO ARREST YOU?

There are three main situations in which you might find yourself attracting the attention of the local police in a Third World country – given you are not a crook. How you react to the prospect of arrest depends entirely on what you might reasonably expect to happen if you don't do anything to resist and go along quietly.

If you are being arrested by a corrupt local police force in the Third World on some trumped-up charges, they probably only want a bribe and you should pay them if you have the cash on you. Otherwise, your family or friends will have to pay your way out after you have been seriously inconvenienced in a cell. Unless, of course, your arrest makes the media and looks bad so you are killed and disposed of to avoid embarrassment to senior officers. While you are awaiting release, you may be beaten with sticks for the amusement of your captors.

In Africa, Europeans are considered by the locals to have money, so the police stop their cars for 'speeding' and will hold them, even cart them off to jail, unless they hand over a few dollars or some cigarettes.

It is also the case that in some places in Africa and the Middle East you are assumed to be the guilty party if you are in a road accident and someone is hurt. The way they think is that if you were not there it would not have happened and their countryman would be fine. So you either pay up on the spot and get away or you suffer in jail for a while until someone does finally pay. The alternative is that you are found guilty and made to suffer until someone pays. And in some countries the locals will throw themselves under the wheels of your car to be able to sue you. Or throw their children.

If you are working on a covert operation gathering industrial or military information and you are arrested in the Third World, you are probably either going to be left to rot as a deniable asset or there will be strings pulled at a diplomatic level, leading to an exchange or other arrangement. This may take some time.

You must make your own judgement as to how strongly you should resist arrest, depending on the country and the situation you find yourself in. Very often police in all countries are friendly so as to avoid resistance right up until the time they have you disarmed and in a cell.

Decide in your head, well in advance, what you will do if things turn difficult, then stick to the plan. If I was in France or Germany and was stopped for speeding or fighting in a bar, I would pay the fine or accept the arrest. If in Spain, I would pay the bribe. In Central Africa, parts of Asia and a great many other places, however, when going into harm's way, if a bribe was not accepted on the spot I would kill any person who tried to arrest me. I would do this because in some places it is standard practice to hold people in terrible conditions and torture them until their company or family pay enough to get them out.

If you are operating undercover or trading in a country where they lock you up and throw away the key at the drop of a hat, the best time to escape is before they have you in custody. If you are involved in a road accident or a bar fight or even if you are robbed, do what it takes to get away from the scene without meeting the police. They may not be as sympathetic as they are in the West.

The first stage of dealing with this situation is to avoid the arrest in the first place. There are a number of precautions you can take:

Use a local driver so he will take the blame if there is an accident.

Do not ever drink alcohol while out in public, especially in Muslim countries.

Try to keep at least one person with you.

Always make sure one person in the group speaks the local language.

Do not offer a target for a pick-pocket.

Do not go into sensitive areas unless your mission demands it.

Once you are arrested, disarmed and inside a genuine prison, the chances of your escape are much slimmer than they are outside, so you have to assess if the escape is worth the risk of death. You do this by considering the odds on your being rescued by the cavalry or released through some kind of diplomatic negotiations, bribery or even being let off. If all of these seem unlikely, you either look for a chance of escape or you are left with a series of techniques to improve your situation inside. These are covered below.

But, before that, let's consider how to avoid arrest. Police and similar types who arrest other people tend to get sloppy. They know they have guns and they know their victims are pretty much always frightened and submissive. All this makes them arrogant and careless.

At the point of arrest you will be in a room somewhere or in a stopped car. This does not make any difference as the only thing of importance is who is watching.

You are not frightened or submissive: you are a lion pretending to be a timid deer. But you do want to look like a deer. Move slowly and awkwardly. Limp if it seems reasonable. Do not look the officer in the eye, look down and only glance in his direction to get your bearings. Stumble or do what it takes to get the officer close to you – in front or behind makes no odds. By this point your body language has confirmed to him that you are no threat – you are afraid and possibly drunk, weak or injured.

The next stage depends on how you are armed and if the officer has his gun drawn. There are many possibilities. So take what serves from the following.

If he is close behind you with his gun out in his right hand, spin anti-clockwise to face him. As you move, step towards him and push his gun away outwards with your left arm. At the same moment strike to his chin with your right hand to render him unconscious. If you have not practised this technique to perfection, instead head-butt him on the nose with your head dipped to avoid damage to you. Step forward and grasp his gun hand with both your hands and, keeping your arms straight, move the gun and his arm in a big circle clockwise over your head. This will turn him to stand bent over, face down with his right arm locked straight. The gun can easily be taken at this point as he cannot grip even if conscious.

If you have a gun accessible from a hip holster and there is no one around, spin as before and step towards him. Place the muzzle against his chest to deaden the noise a little and fire once. No one will react to one single shot. Try it in town. The best option, if you have one, is to use a knife as it is quieter.

If any of this goes wrong do not end up wrestling with him. The object is always to kill or disable quickly before further resistance arrives. Passers-by do not join in if they see someone has been put down but they may if they see a struggle going on.

If you find yourself with his gun in your hands but he is still conscious, be aware that it is not as simple to knock someone out as it seems on TV – except with a punch to the side of the chin. The best way to knock someone out in a struggle is to bang their head against a brick wall. Not a wooden wall or a car. If there is something heavy around, hit him repeatedly over the head with it until he stops moving or breathing.

Then get away quickly. If you have been seen and could be recognised, you will probably have to either get out of the country openly that day or by stealth later. In some countries there are no-go areas where you can hole up indefinitely; it all depends on where you are. Do not get caught after killing a police officer.

## INDUCTION

Now let's look at what might happen when you have decided to accept capture or arrest. When you arrive in an organised state prison there will be an induction process ranging from photographs, fingerprints, body search and uniform issue to being beaten with sticks and thrown in a communal cell. In some countries, particularly in Central America, you will be stripped by the inmates already in the cell, probably at knifepoint.

The people running the show in a POW camp will have a different agenda. What they want is to split the officers from the enlisted men to cut down on organisation and then they will want to interrogate anyone who may have useful information. This means you will be placed in a barracks-like environment, most likely with other enlisted men – or junior officers if you are a Rupert. Senior officers don't get taken prisoner as a rule.

While this is happening, keep quiet, do not get angry and do not make eye contact with your captors. The whole purpose of the exercise is not to be noticed any more than anyone else. By keeping quiet you may avoid damage and this will not only be more comfortable but it will give you more options when it comes to planning an escape.

## KEEPING MONEY

In certain criminal communities around the Mediterranean and in South America, it is a common practice to own a small cylinder which may be opened by a screw-thread or friction and is used to keep money or drugs safe and dry. This is stuffed up the back passage, where it will only be found in a determined search. It cannot easily be stolen without intimidating the owner to relieve himself or cutting it out with a knife. If the device is made of plastic it will not show up easily on an X-ray.

When professionals are looking for things like this, they oblige the prisoner to relieve himself under observation so there is no way it can be retained. If you are likely to find yourself in a prisoner-type situation you might want to consider this option as a fair amount of cash can be carried.

More in some than in others, obviously.

## DEALING WITH INMATES AND GUARDS

In some countries, particularly the USA and Eastern Europe, there will be a hierarchy among prisoners. Effectively there will be a gang united by race, occupation or creed, the leader of which controls the others through fear. If there is a confrontation between you and the leader and you are good enough, you need to kill or cripple him as the remainder will crumble without him. If you cannot do this you need to make a deal somehow so that he sees the benefit in protecting you or at least not robbing you. It is likely that the leader of a prison gang, while he may not be a brain surgeon, will have lots of animal cunning. Remember that criminals lie, cheat and steal for a living and are totally without any honour whatsoever. Do not trust them or believe anything they say as there are a great many techniques among convicts for taking advantage of the inexperienced.

In any prison, things we take for granted become prized possessions. I have known men slashed with knives for the loss of a postage stamp. But then some of the criminals are crazy too.

In a POW camp the situation is generally much better, with a camaraderie among the inmates. There may not even be any ill will from the guards as they are only doing their job and may well take a friendly interest in you if you play it right. Here it always helps if you speak the language but that is up to you. I find languages difficult but I always make the effort to learn the basics wherever I am. Hello, please, thank you, two beers and so on.

As for the guards, in any state-run prison they are low-paid and not too bright. They may have a culture of entertaining themselves by beating or torturing their prisoners; or they may just spit in the tea or worse. The first thing you need to do is avoid antagonising them. You can find out later if they will take a bribe.

The main thing to know about guards is that their job is mind-numbingly boring and they will almost always get sloppy. At the very least you may be able to bargain with them for cigarettes and food if it is possible to get someone on the outside to send them money or gifts.

## TORTURE

A good hiding is not torture and should not be a problem for anyone but a wimp. What does constitute torture is electric shocks to the genitals, which causes convulsions, beating of the soles of the feet with rods, which is more painful than you can imagine, and restriction of breathing by water-boarding, as the Americans do. Water-boarding is when the victim is tied flat on their back to a seesaw-type board which is then tilted to dip his head under the water for a while. Sometimes, a cloth is attached to the face and water poured on it to restrict breathing. Alternatively, a gas mask is placed on a victim's face and the hole where the filter goes is just blocked for a while to prevent breathing. Sometimes a plastic bag is used.

I don't care how tough you are, or what secrets you are trying to keep from the enemy, after four days of any one of the above, you will talk. You will beg them to allow you to incriminate your friends and family if any of those techniques is applied.

There is a certain unit I was involved with, not in the British Army, where we did anti-interrogation training. The only reason I can see for doing this is to encourage soldiers to kill themselves first as no one can handle it for long. We were given a variant on water-boarding where the head was held under water for a while, then released. Eventually it gets so unpleasant you suck in water to try to drown but they bring you round and start again.

A technique is taught, which I will not describe here, whereby you can make yourself unconscious using posture and a breathing trick, but even that only works for a while.

I have said elsewhere that, after not eating for four days, your mind changes so that you find the strangest things appetising, even dog shit. Well, after a few days' torture, your mind changes too, and you will do anything to stop it.

Far better not to get there in the first place.

## RED CROSS PARCELS

Will there be a rescue or a diplomatic deal? First of all, you need to make sure your people know where you are if you possibly can. In some cases this may happen as a matter of course without your doing anything, whereas in others you may have to bribe someone about to be released with the promise of a wedge of cash from your friends when they tell them where you are.

When your friends know about you, they can sometimes bring pressure to bear to improve your situation and treatment and they may even be able to get you released if it is a civilian situation.

With a POW situation one of your dog tags should be taken as ID and returned to your own side, then at least you will be put on the list for visits from the Red Cross or similar.

This is where you have to decide if you are going to sit and wait or make a break. In all probability the accommodation will not be the Hilton and you will get weaker the longer you are held.

## RECONNAISSANCE

If you have decided to escape, or are awaiting the results of communications with the outside to make that decision, you need to take a good look around the place as far as you are able. I should not have to remind you that prisons are made to keep people in. To get out you have to find a flaw in the system and act with determination – probably with little inside support if it is a civilian institution. In a POW camp you may find yourself drawing straws to see who goes first when everyone has been working on an escape plan.

While you are recovering, you can still achieve something. Check what times the guards patrol and change shifts. Try to find out what is beyond the walls you can see. Very often prisoners are used as labour in the laundry or cookhouse. Find out if any of these tasks gets you access to the outside – to receive incoming deliveries, for example. You may need to pay to discover this and pay again to get a plum job.

The most important asset you can get is someone on the outside. Try to make a plan before the worst happens so that there will be someone to help you. On a covert mission you should have someone in the country with no connection to you and who therefore would not have been lifted with you. Once inside, get a message to them as mentioned above, through someone who is released or through a guard. From your contact outside you should be able to get plans of the prison, a mobile phone or similar and some cash to bribe the guards. Enough money will get you out of anywhere. In the Third World this need not be a fortune.

## TUNNELS AND OTHER SCHEMES

Escape plans are where detention as a POW is totally different from being held as a civilian prisoner. In a POW situation it should be possible to get a group of men together to work on an escape and then draw lots for a smaller number to escape or at least go first. You will not be short of people to do reconnaissance, dig holes, file through bars and so on.

Among criminals this will not happen. Criminals are not in prison for nothing, even if every one of them has a story as to why they were wrongly accused. If you have not been in a civilian prison, I will tell you that every single inmate has a series of stories to use depending on who he is talking to. If another criminal, it will show how big a crook he is and how clever. If he is talking to someone who doesn't know the ropes or who he suspects of being a spy, it will show how he was wrongly convicted. Take it from me, the people you meet in prison, almost without exception, are low-life vermin with no morals whatsoever. Even if you bribe them, they will most likely take the bribe then turn you in for another favour from the management.

## MAKING YOUR MOVE

When you do actually move, it must be with full commitment. Try to arrange things so that you get as long as possible before they come looking for you. The obvious way to do this is leave in the evening but do what it takes.

If you are caught trying to escape, they will not thank you for making the effort. Most prisons move those who try to escape to much less pleasant accommodation which is even more difficult to escape from. If you have hurt a warden they will at the very least give you the hiding of your life and most likely kill you.

This is why you act harmless and quiet so as not to be thought a security risk. Then, when you do move, you move fast and hard. You must gamble everything on one turn of the card.

If you break out of prison, people are going to come looking for you. How they do this depends entirely on the situation of the prison and the society. If you are out in the country it may be dogs, search teams and helicopters. If you are in a city it may be possible to blend into some rough quarter where the police don't go.

The best possible option is to have a mate waiting for you with suitable transport – fly you out in a microlight or whatever.

One of the things you must consider at this point is, do they really have an idea where I am? If they don't, a booby-trap to slow the pursuit is definitely not a good idea as all it will do is give them a rough idea of where you have got to or what direction you are taking.

## Chapter Four

# Escape From A Hostage Situation

Imagine a bunch of crooks or religious crazies are holding you hostage or trying to take you hostage. From where I am sitting there is no obvious difference between taking someone hostage and kidnapping them. Perhaps some media types with an agenda not entirely hostile to the kidnappers started using the word 'hostage' to make it sound less criminal and a little more acceptable.

Whatever you call it, snatching people and holding them, whether for money, to force action from politicians or to gain media coverage, is pretty low on the scale of human endeavour. The kidnappers are playing on the suffering of the victims and their families to get what they want.

From your point of view, being taken hostage is one of the worst things that can happen to you. The problem is that if the kidnappers want money it is easier and safer to take the ransom and then kill you so you cannot talk and do not have to be handed over.

If they want their comrades released, or your politicians to change their policy, the chances of your survival are remote because the people making the decisions do not give a rat's arse about you or your family. To be fair, though, non-cooperation with kidnappers is better for everyone in the long run as it makes a risky operation totally unprofitable for the criminals and therefore they will not do it. Every kidnapper who is paid, or deal that is done, sows the seeds for the next crop of victims. Of course, it is easy to say that so long as it is no one you care about, and you have to sympathise with wealthy families who pay ransoms.

If the bastards want publicity, it is going to get gruesome. Taking you prisoner then keeping you alive for months on end is one big photo opportunity to get their name in lights. In the end, when you have been kept in chains for a long, long time, they are going to kill you messily so it makes the TV news. Someone once said, 'Any publicity is good publicity,' and sadly that is how it works for political kidnappers. There should be an international ban on doing deals with them and on mentioning them on TV. It is the only way to stop them.

Because the odds of survival as a hostage are so low, it is worth taking almost any trouble or risk to avoid becoming one. Hostage taking by criminals is normally referred to as kidnap and in some countries, such as Italy and Colombia, it is not as uncommon as you might think. Most kidnappees are killed eventually either to avoid them identifying the criminals or because they have got the money.

There are some differences in dealing with kidnappers

doing it for money and kidnappers doing it for political or religious reasons and we will deal with these as we go along but the important thing to remember is that you are almost certainly going to die unless you escape. Fortunately, there is a fair chance of a successful escape if you follow these instructions.

If you are taken prisoner or hostage by Muslim terrorists – which, to be frank, is the most likely scenario for a soldier – your odds of survival, if you do not escape, are not good. You will be kept alive for propaganda purposes, but when this aim has been achieved you will almost certainly be killed, very messily and possibly on camera.

So, particularly in this latter situation, it is better to fight to the last round than surrender, and after the last round there are still alternatives. A friend of mine was wounded while being pursued through the bush in Angola. He could no longer run and the enemy were closing. If he was lucky he would be hacked to death by the men, if not he would be handed over to the women and they might keep him alive for days or even weeks. What he did was take a pin from a grenade and hold the grenade to his head. Release the lever and check out free of charge. Clean and easy if you are not one of those timid souls who want to live for ever.

As with the arrest and imprisonment situation, the easiest time to get away is before you are caught. Once you are captured, the sooner you make a move the better, as your captors are likely to get better organised and you are likely to get weaker.

Again, once captured, you need to assess if you are going to be kept alive and if so what the chances are of a rescue or eventual release. What you do if you are taken hostage entirely depends on who it is that has you, what they hope to gain by holding you and what the people in the outside world they are talking to do about it.

## AVOIDING BEING A TARGET

The best way to deal with kidnapping is to not even get on their radar.

In a civilian situation in a First World country, you are only a target if you are from a very wealthy family or you are a big noise in a big company, so in either case take security advice. What this will amount to is: keep bodyguards around, don't follow routines, don't pick up a tail coming away from home and a few other pointers. The whole idea is to make yourself more difficult to take than equally valuable targets so that the crooks go for an easier target.

Bodyguards are not really there to win a shootout, despite what you see on TV. If it comes to a shooting match, they have not really done their job. What should happen when you have company is that no one will try to snatch you – they will go for someone who is less of a challenge. Your guards should also be advising you where not to go in town and so on. The trouble is that, if kidnappers do decide to take you even though you have guards, they will come in heavy-handed and kill them first. This means they are ready for trouble and more difficult for you to deal with.

If you choose to go as a civilian to somewhere like Somalia or Ethiopia or certain parts of the Middle East, you have only yourself to blame if some local bandit takes it into his head to hold you for ransom. But, assuming you have to work in a country where you are a target, follow the rules above with the addition that for the limited period of your visit it might be worth changing your appearance at intervals or when you go to the loo. Wigs and false moustaches may sound silly but, if you're being tailed and you pop into a bar, change in the boys' room and walk out by another entrance, you may well lose them. Of course, this is SOP for meetings of significance anyway.

Suppose for some reason you don't have bodyguards present and a couple of villains try to take you. If you are in a trouble spot you should be armed and wearing lightweight body armour sufficient to stop a knife or pistol bullet. This can easily be worn under a suit jacket or similar without being obvious, although to be fair it is unpleasantly warm in a sunny climate.

Just like with arrest, aim not to appear any sort of threat. Unlike arrest, there will most likely be no request to go along quietly. What normally happens is that either you are grabbed and bodily thrown into a waiting vehicle or a gun is put to your ribs and you are ordered to go with them.

If anything is put over your mouth, it is likely to be chloroform or a similar drug to knock you out. You have until you need to breathe to do something about this. This might sound a little sudden but we are not training your grandmother here – we expect readiness and reaction on your part.

If someone grabs you from behind, slouch down then head-butt backwards and stamp on their instep. Turn and strike with your fist to the jaw or knife to the belly, or draw and fire at the centre of target. If you haven't come across the term 'centre of target' before, it means aim for a point halfway from the top to the bottom and halfway across the observed target on the basis that you are more likely to hit it somewhere. You can go for an 'arty' shot when your target goes down. Try the same pistol manoeuvre as explained in the previous chapter as lightweight armour stops bullets, but it feels like being hit with a baseball bat.

Unless they are expecting you to resist, as I have just suggested you will almost certainly come out on top, provided you are not facing a huge number of opponents.

## RESCUE OR NOT?

If you are taken in a civilian kidnapping or by terrorists, someone is quickly going to miss you and tell the police or military as appropriate. The trouble is that, while the record for recovering hostages is good, the record for recovering them alive is very bad.

So, if you just sit still, the odds on your being released are not at all attractive. If criminals have you there is doubt the money will be offered, if it is offered it may not get there and if it gets to the kidnappers they may well kill you anyway. If this is a military or political situation, the odds are pretty much the same as your release depends on your government releasing other terrorists or pulling out of a war or similar. And they're going to do that to save your arse, aren't they? If you are in the hands of terrorists, you have a very slim chance that intelligence might pick up where you are being held, storm the place and get you out alive. It has happened, but don't hold your breath.

In 1976, an Air France passenger plane carrying 250

people was hijacked by Palestinian terrorists as it flew from Israel to Paris. The aircraft was diverted to Entebbe in Uganda, where the terrorists were supported by the dictator Idi Amin. To cut a long story short, a team of heroic Israelis set off to Africa and took down a quarter of the Ugandan air force before beating a small army of Ugandans who were guarding the hostages, killing all the terrorists and escaping with most of the hostages alive. The leader of the operation on the ground was Lieutenant Colonel Yonatan Netanyahu and he was shot dead by a Ugandan soldier while leading from the front, as Israeli officers tend to do. What a way to go, though!

In Iran, an embassy full of Americans was held for 444 days between November 1979 and January 1981 by 'students' in support of the Iranian revolution, and the hostages could not be extracted despite the massive power and skill of the US forces. These troops tried unsuccessfully to get them out with Operation Eagle Claw, in which eight servicemen died.

In July 2008, a couple of heroic agents planted among the FARC terrorists in Colombia managed to trick them into allowing their hostages on to a chopper and away to freedom.

This is where you have to decide if you are going to sit and wait for a rescue which may never come or take your fate in your own hands and make a break for it.

## SETTLING IN

If you are captured because you were unprepared, I am tempted to tell you to get on with it but I won't. Probably by car or van, but one way or another, you are going to be taken to a place where the kidnappers feel safe from prying eyes. What sort of place this is depends entirely on the situation you are in.

If the kidnappers are criminals in the West, it might be a rented house in a suburb or anywhere with no close neighbours to see you come in or overhear anything they shouldn't. If they are religious nuts or any other sort of terrorist, you might be taken out into the jungle, taken to a part of town they control or even handed over to a government that pretends to be on the side of the good guys. Who is to know? Wherever they choose to take you, it is a pound to a penny they will make sure you do not know where you are going or where you are when you arrive. If possible, keep your ears open for clues on the way.

Whatever your fate here, the point is that there will be a small number of people guarding you on a rota of some kind. If they are criminals they may only be keeping you alive long enough to make a telephone call or recording. If they are terrorists anything could happen. You need to take your own circumstances into account when you decide how much of a chance is big enough to be worth taking.

Hopefully some sort of routine will be established for your sleep and for feeding and exercising you. If not don't expect to survive long, and make your plans accordingly. But if they do seem set for the long haul then you have a few options.

There is almost no chance of reasoning or negotiating with your captors for release, so don't waste your breath. Try to appear weaker than you are, which may not be difficult as you will probably get weaker anyway from lack of food, exercise or beatings. With luck, your captors may also weaken and, more importantly, they may get sloppy.

It is quite likely that the youngest or weakest of your captors will be given the job of guarding you at night or when no one else wants to do it. At such a time work on him to try to discover where you are so that you know what you will be up against if you get out. Also try to make a friend of the person, however revolting you might find him. By matching his opinions, posture and breathing so far as possible, you may just build up enough of a relationship to lower his guard a notch.

At this point, I want to mention what is officially called the Stockholm Syndrome. I am not going into all the psychobabble that the shrinks use to explain it but what it amounts to is a psychological change that comes over some people when they are kidnapped. It was first made famous in Sweden in 1973 when bank robbers held hostages for nearly a week. At the end of that period some of the hostages actually felt sympathy for their abusers and tried to defend them. I know it sounds pretty crazy but it is true that this does sometimes happen, so watch out for feeling sympathy for your captors – it is not you doing the thinking.

If you have decided to escape or are awaiting the results of comms to make that decision, you need to take as good a look around the place as you can. Again, take note of guard changes and regular events such as mealtimes and toilet breaks if any. Listen carefully for clues to where you are and what might be waiting for you outside if you cannot actually see the outdoors.

You will be very fortunate indeed to have any prisoner for company who is both uninjured and game for an escape attempt. More likely you will be alone or, failing that, with some weepy toe-rag: the chances of terrorists being able to take and hold a bunch of real soldiers is slim indeed. The point is that if you are alone you are the only one your captors have to watch and take care of. If you have company but they are not game you not only have to escape but also to take the decision to abandon your companions, and this is not always clear-cut. You may also have to escape against their wishes, and bear in mind that they may squeal to your captors to save their own necks. If you are not sure of support among your companions, it is better to keep your own counsel and say nothing at all of your plans.

When you do move, it must be all or nothing. Failure is not something to think about for too long as the result will be unpleasant. Once you are ready to move, then escape or die trying, as either outcome will be a better option by far than being caught and living.

If you were kidnapped for money, you could be anywhere but the good news is that if you can get away you have a very good chance of not being recaptured. In fact, you may well not be pursued at all as the bad guys may be running in the opposite direction.

But if this is a political or religious operation the chances are you will be either in the jungle or a slum sympathetic to the terrorists. So you are either going to be chased or will meet hostility from the locals. If you are pursued across country by terrorists, exactly the same rules apply as for a military situation. Set booby-traps if you can and run faster if you cannot.

Having escaped you will almost certainly be unequipped and unarmed unless you were able to steal something. The old footfall trap, where you dig a hole and put a sharpened spike in the bottom, is about the best you can do without munitions or tools, and that would take some effort with a blunt stick, so in fact you are probably better just moving as fast as you can. If you have the choice, try to cross hard ground as it makes tracking difficult.

# Chapter Five

# Escape From
# A Mob

Let's now look at what to do when a mob forms around you bent on hanging you from a lamppost. It is one of the trickier situations which can come about when your armoured car hits a mine, when you are on the road working or doing business or spying in plain clothes and your cover is blown, or even when you are a student in a foreign bar and a woman screams.

I nearly came up against a mob in my early teens while riding pillion on a mate's motorbike. We were passing through a pretty rough area of a town in the north of England when a little boy ran out from behind a parked car. The bike hit him – a glancing blow as there was no way to avoid him – and the child went down. My friend stopped and we ran to help the child. Pretty much as soon as we got there, men and women arrived seemingly from nowhere and they were not happy. They wanted someone to blame and we were handy. Luckily, my mate was a very big guy and the balance just tipped in our favour with the crowd deciding against trying to lynch us.

I think coming up against a mob is about the most scary thing you can face. Far worse than any sort of fire-fight because of the sheer vicious, mindless rage in the people. It has happened to me many times in a whole range of circumstances since and every time there is that chill in your belly that says your body is afraid for its life.

Do you remember the film *Black Hawk Down*? It was based on the true story of a US chopper coming down in a town full of very unfriendly Ethiopians. A mob formed and they did all manner of nasty things to the crew – both to those who were initially alive and those who were not. If your vehicle is hit by an IED, or improvised explosive device, such as a roadside bomb, or shot up by a sniper in town, right afterwards a crowd will gather who are likely to want to finish you off. In Iraq, they will bring their own petrol bombs. You may have seen the news clip of the British soldiers being pelted by petrol bombs after their armoured vehicle was disabled.

If you are going to work undercover among people who are not your friends, there is always the chance your cover will be blown and trouble will kick off in a bar, a store or anywhere really. Working as a soldier you will do endless foot patrols among people who would like to see you dead. If you get enough people together and something sets them off, they will turn on you and you'll be torn apart like the Red Caps (British Military Police) were in southern Iraq recently. Lastly, if you are travelling the world, by definition you will be among strangers, people from a different culture, and, while my experience is that people everywhere are pretty decent when they don't have a reason to hate you, if something goes wrong, like a wallet is stolen or a woman starts screaming, you are the one they will turn on. So you do need to know how to deal with this situation.

Given the way mobs make me feel uncomfortable, and the fact a fair few have had a go at me, I have thought about them a lot and the conclusion I have come to is that there is a primitive instinct in ordinary people which, when activated by the sort of situation we're talking about, turns them into a sort of group demon. Perfectly ordinary people will howl for your blood and beat you to a pulp with rocks or iron bars and when they come round they just don't know what came over them. In the grip of this impulse people lose all sense, all fear and all morals. It is just like when there is a breakdown of law and order in some places, for instance when the electric supply fails, and people smash their way into stores and carry off anything they can lay their hands on.

My first real experience of mobs was in Northern Ireland, where initially I worked in a snatch squad during riots with the job of running out from the line of shields into the crowd and grabbing the troublemakers. Good job, hey? We worked in pairs and I won't give out my buddy's name here as he is the sort to keep quiet about what he does. I haven't seen him for years but he is one of the nicest guys you could wish to meet. A welder in civilian life, he joined the army, as many young men do, for a bit of adventure. The unusual thing about him was that he was devoted to a form of martial art which could be described as 'soft'. There is no punching or kicking or anything fancy but the guy just seems to take hold of someone gently by the hand and lead them around in circles or flip them around and break their limbs or throw them at walls. His party piece was that at his club, among others of his kind, he would invite someone to have a hack at him with a samurai sword and he – I kid you not – would catch this between the palms of his hands. Handy man to have around in a rough bar.

There weren't riots every day in Northern Ireland during the Troubles but when there were they really kicked off. The Irish of both persuasions are lovely people by and large but when the mob thing gripped them they were fearsome.

A couple of our guys in plain clothes were watching an IRA funeral, sitting in a little Renault 5, I think it was. Someone in the crowd on the lookout for strangers spotted them and so, having done the secret squirrel tricky driving course, they did the old 'J' turn, a reverse handbrake turn, and tried to get away. Trouble was, all the black cabs in Northern Ireland are Catholic and they were forming a sort of cordon. They moved in a group to block all escape and the little Renault was stuck. That is another argument for driving a big, heavy motor.

Moments later the crowd got there, having turned into a mob on the way. They began beating on the roof of the little car with iron bars and then the windows went. One of the men inside drew his pistol and fired a couple of warning shots but it was over in seconds and they were dragged out. One was beaten to death on the spot and the other was dragged to some wasteland and beaten to a pulp with iron bars. All under the watching eyes of a security helicopter unable to fire into the crowd.

This is the sort of thing you only need to experience once to remember. If a bunch of people are after your blood, expect no mercy and do what needs to be done to get away. Here's what to do.

## WORKING UNDERCOVER

One of the best ways to become the target of a mob is to work undercover among the enemies of our way of life. It is easy to get the idea that being a secret squirrel is exiting and glamorous from the movies and TV. In the real world, working undercover is just a stressful hard slog. There is no connection whatsoever with what you see on TV.

What sort of work could you be doing? The obvious kind is infiltrating a terrorist cell but when Muslims are involved that is tricky. You need to be of the same or similar race to really avoid suspicion and there are few from the Indian subcontinent who are on our side. The next best option is to be African as there are lots of African Muslims.

For an anti-terrorist operation, you need a plausible excuse to get inside the group. This in itself is tricky as the decentralised system employed by, say, Al-Qaida uses long-time friends from the same mosque so they know each other well and can trust one another to die at the right time. Sometimes, and this is SOP for all sorts of intelligence cells, they are recruited, selected without putting themselves forward, from a suitably qualified group. A group of Save-the-Whale fund-raisers would be a good place to recruit people you wanted to mine whaling ships, wouldn't it? Of course, this is why the intelligence services plant sleepers in all organisations of this type.

What happens with the terrorist cell system, when it is done right, is that the recruiter selects his people and approaches them. The recruiter is always a stranger but vouched for by their religious leader. If they seem keen, they are tested by ordering them to do something unlawful, and this is often filmed so as to have a control on them. Killing a member of the opposition or firebombing their home is an obvious test. Only then are they introduced to other members of their group. Then comes the clever part: the recruiter disappears, leaving them only a way of contacting an unknown controller. This is how a sleeper cell of people loyal to the cause is established. It is very difficult to crack as who would dare arrest a religious leader without solid evidence, and even then... Once set up, the cell may be left undisturbed or just kept simmering until needed.

The important part of this system, you will understand, is that these disposable volunteers, the cannon fodder of the terrorist movement, can be arrested and interrogated because they will not be able to give any information about their organisation above cell level. The officers, the brains of the outfit, remain safe. So all the controller has to do is arrange training for them, have them collect materials for bombs or whatever and point them at the target of his choice.

The group always has a secure means of communication with its controller. Sometimes this is by telephone or internet but these means are far less secure than most people think. I have to be careful here not to say too much as I don't want to help the bad guys but they know a lot more than people think already, so I can say something. And be sure we have ways of finding out what they are doing. Very often they are allowed to continue training and even carrying out operations for a very long time until our people have the entire network in the bag. British defensive intelligence, MI5, are very, very good at this.

What I can say is that the intelligence services use false recruiters to set up their own cells for their own purposes. So, if you are a supporter of terrorism, be aware that when you are approached it may not be a terrorist and you may be lining up for a life sentence in high security. Fun, hey?

Another situation you might find yourself in is spying. And I'm not joking here: the targets for our spying efforts are a lot more mundane than you might think. Oh, yes, we want pictures of the latest aircraft the opposition have but don't you think satellites can do that every day of the week? No, what the man on the ground is tasked with obtaining is information about military technical equipment or civilian equipment which may have a military bearing such as nuclear-reactor parts or machinery for producing weapons and things of this nature.

Sometimes a senior sort of businessman leaving for a trip abroad will be approached by our intelligence people and asked to look out for something or someone on his trip. You can be sure our team already know a lot more than they are saying and more likely than not they will be looking for confirmation of their suspicions. This sort of job can be a little risky.

What real professional spies do is a little different from the movies. They work out of our embassy in the country concerned and have diplomatic immunity. Rather than trying to get into the places and positions where the target information is held, like you might see in a James Bond movie, they approach local people who already have access. These are then set up in embarrassing situations with women, or men, and photographed for blackmail. They may also be bribed but more likely both stick and carrot are used, just to make sure.

Again, communicating with your own people under the watch of the local government is the tricky part and this is achieved by letter drops and similar means, to avoid radio and phone taps. In 2006, our people in Russia were caught with egg on their faces but, as often is the case, the diplomats and MI6 got away and the local recruits went to jail. What happened was our people had set up a Russian spy in a military enterprise and got him to collect classified information on a sort of computer memory stick. What he had to do then was download this on to a computer in a Moscow park disguised as a rock. Really! I understand a certain local British diplomat could not account for £300,000 in paid cheques so the offer may have been tempting.

This plan worked quite well, with the local recruit walking his dog in the area on a regular basis to provide cover. Unfortunately, our MI6 operators were sloppy, unusually, and allowed themselves to be followed for some weeks and to be seen unloading the 'rock'. The next time the spy turned up he was lifted by the modern equivalent of the KGB and caught red-handed with all the info and means of passing it over. No argument. He is now rotting in prison while our people were just deeply embarrassed.

The last situation I'll consider here, and the most likely for my readers, is that you are on the edge of our secret squirrel network, perhaps in the military, and have been given the job of hanging about a certain house, office or market disguised as a local and looking for a certain person. I have done this so many times and I promise you it is almost as boring as sitting in a sangar (a fortified observation position) watching an empty street. Of course there is the fear to keep you on your toes.

If you find yourself in any of these jobs and you are discovered, the bad guys find they are in a tricky position. Very often they do not want us to know what they know and sometimes they do not want to be seen to be against us, so they will not just shoot you. What they will often do is call up the local rent-a-mob and have you torn limb from limb. 'Oh yes, it looks like he assaulted a woman and the crowd set on him.'

If you are old enough, you may remember a real British Army hero called Captain Robert Nairac. He was only 27 when he died. His job was to spend time in certain bars used by supporters of the IRA in the bandit country near the border between Northern Ireland and the Republic. He did his homework and fitted in well, even singing republican songs on the stage at the Three Steps public house in South Armagh. Somehow his cover was blown, perhaps by attracting too much attention and getting a detailed check, and he was discovered. The IRA beat him to within an inch of his life, then took him away and tortured him with electric drills and other unpleasantness for some days before shooting him. He did not talk but died with a Catholic prayer on his lips. A salute for Captain Nairac, George Cross.

## HOW MOBS WORK

A mob, for the purpose of this explanation, is a group of people who have come together in a state of excitement to achieve one aim. Usually a lynching. This is quite different from a riot in which the people take advantage of a power cut to loot the local stores or where they are facing a line of troops who are ordered not to shoot them all, as described below.

But these three situations all seem to feed off the same strange instinct which lurks in apparently ordinary people waiting for the right circumstances to turn them into monsters. In England, if the electricity supply failed on a big scale, people would probably form an orderly queue for candles but in less civilised places people will come out on to the streets and when together in a large group they seem to lose all sense of what is right and wrong, all sense of self-control. They just start smashing things and helping themselves to what they want. Of course, the media will say the poor things were disadvantaged and discriminated against, but the bottom line is that they are stealing from the rest of society and this is not acceptable. Looters should be shot.

A riot takes place when the forces of law and order are held back for political reasons. Think about it. A few thousand demonstrators are facing a line of police or soldiers. They start throwing rocks and petrol bombs and the police or service personnel stand there and take it to a great extent. Why? Because they are ordered to. The way it works is this: if you have a big crowd of people it will make the news. They can do pretty much what they want at the time and it will be much later that the ringleaders and worst offenders are arrested. At the time, the powers that be do not want to be seen as heavy-handed and turn the majority of the people against them, as surely would happen if the demonstrators were shot; no, they keep public sympathy by using the police or military as targets for the demonstrators' aggression.

To be fair, there has to be some sort of balance in a society between keeping order and people who are very unhappy with the order which is being kept. To some extent, protests are a way of letting off steam and making your views felt, so I feel they are acceptable provided they do not go too far. Without the freedom to protest, it would be a fascist state where everyone has to do as they are told without feedback or argument, and a few riots are far better than such slavery, don't you think?

So riots only happen where the forces of law and order can be relied upon not to shoot the rioters. Like kicking a big fierce dog with a muzzle on. Believe me, I have seen this countless times.

The sort of mob we are talking about here, though, is a little different. Mostly it is a spontaneous gathering of people all with the same feelings about a situation. If they are poor and you are a rich-looking foreigner, you are a target for resentment in some places. If you dress differently from the locals and so can be seen not to be a member of their religion you are a target. If you don't speak the language they can say anything about you and you have no answer. And, of course, if you are a soldier on duty in a town keeping the locals down, they are not going to feel very well disposed towards you. All it takes is a trigger to set them off.

The trigger could be something or nothing depending on how strong the local feelings are and how firmly they are being held down. It could be something as simple as a woman screaming next to you and the men all assume you have done something wrong. In some places there are prostitutes who will approach foreigners and threaten to scream if they are not paid. You could be in a traffic accident where a local is injured and the crowd turn nasty. Or you could be on patrol in the market and someone throws a stone at you. Everyone else will join in and what do you do?

## HOW TO AVOID MOBS

The most obvious way to avoid mobs is not be there of course, but sometimes you have to, so what then? Every situation is different but from what I have said already you should have a good idea of how a mob situation is set off and therefore how not to set it off.

If you are operating dressed as a civilian, for genuine or other reasons, there is the usual chance of something like a traffic accident sparking mob action. In this case you should not be driving but have a local person drive you, or at least someone who speaks the local language. Then, if something happens, you are not the focus and the local may be able to calm things down with words. When spending time in bars, always try to have someone to watch your back, stay sober and always have an interpreter if you possibly can.

If you are in uniform, don't stare at the local women – or camels in some places – as this may cause offence. Though the local beggars and kids may be a real pain day after day, never kick them away as this can upset people looking to be upset. Do not buy anything from the locals as one day one of them will claim you are robbing him. Try to keep out of the most crowded areas when you have a say in what you do.

If a mob forms around you and you can't run, try to take up a position with a wall behind you. When you are in a group, having only one flank to protect will effectively give you twice the men to face the mob, and when you are alone it will protect your back and give you something to lean on. What happens is that the threatening crowd often comes right up against you jeering and yelling without actually trying to kill you to begin with. This is the most dangerous point as in a moment it can turn from a shouting match to someone sticking a knife in your ribs or hitting you over the head with a rock.

In a military situation fixed bayonets are a fine deterrent to this sort of excessive intimacy as they can slip into someone without the use of firearms. If this is not practical or fails, the team leader should fire a few shots into the air. In some places this will have everyone running away because they are either not used to gunfire or a shot means someone is being killed. But in situations where the people are used to gunfire, or more excitable, all hell will break loose.

Very often the people at the front don't want shooting so they won't do much more than yell but someone at the back will throw a rock, then another and another. If you are not wearing a helmet, a rock can be as deadly as a bullet but even if it is not fatal a rock to the head means a man down and the crowd will come in and kick him to death.

Going down on the floor is one of the main things to avoid, as I said above. With your back against a wall you have something to lean on to counter the press of the crowd so you don't get pushed over. It is absolutely vital to stay on your feet as even the most timid rioter will put the boot into any poor sod who goes down.

If things escalate to rocks and people pressing in on you, toss a grenade over their heads and use them as cover. This will take the edge off almost any crowd's excitement. There are certain towns where my friends and I used to go out drinking where we would always carry a pistol and a grenade clipped to the belt. A crowd may not be impressed by a pistol shot but a grenade will take the wind out of their sails.

If you are in civilian clothes or even working as a civilian, you have to make your own decisions about what to carry but a pistol is a comfort in many situations – like when the pimps come hammering on the door when you are still doing business with some young lady.

Assuming the mob is coming for you and you are not going to get away quietly, the first thing to do is identify the leaders and take them down. This applies to a determined riot as well as to a mob trying to lynch you. In a riot situation, look for the ringleaders on the ground, as the real leaders will never be there. Pick out the one doing the shouting and kill them. A mate of mine was in Malaya a long time ago when a proper riot broke out. To follow this story you need to understand that a fire order follows a correct sequence just like any other military communication. In this case, depending which army you are in, it's something like, 'Gun group [who you are talking to], 500 [range to set their sites to] enemy position left of house [where the target is] 50 rounds in bursts: FIRE!' My mate was a young marine and still laughs that his first fire order to his team was: 'Section, the big bastard in the yellow shirt: fire!' A roar of fire from the whole team blew the chap to bits and calmed the situation significantly. As you may imagine.

So the idea is to act firmly and do something to shock the mob into thinking twice about what they are trying to do. If you can do this to the leader, it will have far more effect as there will no longer be someone egging them on.

Once, in my twenties, I was home on leave and went to see a friend of mine in his DIY shop. He was out on business so I settled down to wait, taking a look around the shelves. A little later, his mum, who was minding the shop, came over to me most upset. She took me to the window and pointed at a young man beating the head of another on the pavement and hysterically demanded I do something about it. I really did not want to interfere but I was obliged. I went outside and just told the chap on top – they were only teenagers – to get off and leave the other guy alone. He did so, muttering, and they went away while I went back in the shop.

A few minutes later a mob of around 50 young men came walking down the road towards the shop. When they arrived, they began taking lumps of wood out of a display outside. I realised at this point they were all from the local branch of an agency which supposedly trains young criminals to do something useful. NACRO, I think it was.

At this point, his mum went ballistic, yelling at me to get out of the shop or it would be wrecked. Quite probably, I thought. Me too. Fortunately the first to enter the shop as I made for the door was the ringleader, a tall young man with a very big mouth which he was using to threaten me. I don't take threats well so I just hit him once on the point of the jaw and he went down like a sack of potatoes. Following up on the shock value, I went outside to ask aggressively who was next, and they backed off. Obviously they could have torn me to pieces but shock and taking the initiative are the best you can do in a situation like this.

To sum up, if the crowd turns into a mob, you have to do whatever is needed to take the initiative and get them on the back foot. Almost always, in response to a firm action suitable to the circumstances, the mob will back off and lose their unity of purpose. This might mean smacking the leader or it might mean shooting him, or it might mean a grenade among them all.

## RUNNING FROM A MOB

Once you have broken up the mob in this way, they will not be a further problem in most cases, provided you act quickly. Move away quietly and steadily without giving them something to chase, because, just like any dog, they will chase you if you run.

About the worst thing that can happen is when the best you can do only makes the mob catch their breath and they come forward again. This means a shooting match if you are both armed, so go in hard and do what it takes. On no account, when faced by an armed crowd, think you can just shoot one and walk away. There will always be at least one who wants to make a fight of it and you will be cut to pieces. The ones who don't want to fight will run. Shoot anyone who does not run.

If you have reached the stage where the mob refused to calm down after you hurt their leader, and then it turns out they are not going to run at a little gunfire, you are on a hiding to nothing if you stay. I cannot recommend your chances if you choose to stand and shoot into a bunch of civilians, however hard they are trying to kill you. Afterwards, they will claim they were unarmed and the media will make mincemeat of you. This will be followed by your commanders sacrificing you to the press by locking you up for a very long time. This has already happened to a fair few US troops in Iraq even though US Army leaders tend to stand up for their men.

Let's now consider what you do in this and the other situations we've looked at.

## Part Two

# How To Stay Free When People Are Hunting You

OK, so you have got out of your crashed chopper and escaped from the people who shot it down. Or you have broken contact with the guys who wiped out your patrol. Or you have escaped from the jail or hostage takers. In a mob situation, which we've just dealt with in the previous chapter, the pursuit stage does not last long – one way or another. Now what do you do?

## Chapter Six

# Assessing Your Situation

If the last few minutes have been a little hairy, you need to let the adrenalin subside and think clearly before you do anything else. Better to start moving in the right direction in a few minutes than have to turn around later after wasting time and energy. Try to sit down, take a smoke or brew up if you are organised enough to have the necessary with you and not obviously pressed to keep going.

If you are taken hostage by crooks in your home country, all you have to do after escaping is contact the authorities, as the crooks are most likely moving rapidly in the opposite direction. In every other situation, there are going to be some very unfriendly people looking for you and/or chasing you with intent to do you harm.

Though it is pleasant and comfortable to have all the fancy gear, remember that the most important things you need to get you home are a cool head and determination. You can steal everything else.

What you need to do now is set your course for home,

giving all due thought to avoiding anyone who is chasing you and how you are going to travel. First you need to assess your situation rationally by asking yourself a number of key questions.

## HOW CLOSE ARE THE BAD GUYS?

After the initial kick-off in which you have broken direct line-of-sight pursuit, there are now two possibilities. The people who want your company so badly are either in direct pursuit of you, in which case they are tracking you, or, having lost your tracks, they are searching for you.

In a moment we'll look at how you deal with both of these alternatives, when we have considered who may be doing the tracking or searching. For the present just be aware that if you are being tracked you are in a serious hurry, whereas if all you have to worry about is a search party, then it could be a long way behind. Very often the reality is that the people who are after you have a good idea which way you went but are searching that area either without a direct line of tracks to follow or without the ability to track efficiently.

## WHO IS CHASING ME?

If you are very lucky this might be no one. The one good thing about mobs is that they do not have any stamina and like a sight-hound they lose interest when you are lost from view. The more likely situation is that your pursuers are something between a band of terrorists, the local police force and/or the military of a whole country. The answer to this question tells you what sort of trouble your pursuers will go to and how long they will keep trying.

A band of terrorists might give up after a few hours and get back to their women or goats, whereas a national organisation, once set in motion, will go on for many days or indefinitely and may involve helicopters and many troops searching checkpoints, roadblocks and so on if you are interesting enough.

So you have to weigh up how important you are to the people who want you, what they could do if they wanted and what they probably will do given what they know. If you are carrying a memory stick with incriminating evidence of their nuclear research, don't expect the government to give up any time soon. If you have just run from a shooting match, the winning side may be getting drunk or testing their drug of choice in celebration of their victory.

Who they are, how keen they are, how near they are and, most of all, what resources they have all need to be considered when you make your plan to get you home.

## IS THERE ANY WAY I CAN CALL
## FOR AN EXTRACTION?

No matter what your situation there is nothing so comforting as the thrumming noise of friendly chopper blades approaching to give you a lift home. Is there any way your commanders could know where you are? Do you have a homing beacon you can trigger now – or later when the fuss dies down? Will there be people looking for you from the air so an 'H' spread on the ground may hitch you a lift?

The answer to this tells you how long you have to stay in front of the people chasing you. Either until the cavalry arrives, until the opposition lose interest or until you get out of enemy territory. If you have a taxi coming, you can drop all your kit and run your heart out to make the RV (rendezvous) or keep ahead of the pursuit. If you don't have anyone coming to pick you up, you need to pace yourself for the long haul and carry what you need to keep you going: water, food, weapons and so on.

## WHERE DO I HAVE TO GET TO UNDER MY OWN STEAM?

How far is it and what is the country like? Do I just have to stay free until the chopper gets here, do I have to make it a few clicks (kilometres) to an RV, as that is the closest they can put it down, or do I have to make my way to a distant border or coast?

The answer to this question tells you what risks you are going to have to take in stealing transport and food. As a general rule you should tread as lightly as you can while on the run. Do without food and transport if you can do so without weakening your chances of survival, because every theft of supplies or equipment brings a risk. Risk of capture at the time and risk of narrowing down the search area.

This is where you make decisions about taking the risk of stealing transport and/or food if the opportunity presents itself.

## WHAT CONDITION AM I IN?

How fit am I and do I have any injuries? You should know how many kilometres a day you can do over rough ground. Over hills and carrying a pack, you should be able to maintain four clicks per hour, 12 hours a day, indefinitely. Unless you have a deadline to make an RV, or people are close behind, you should conserve your energy and keep plodding away.

If an injury is slowing you down, you have to make a decision between waiting for it to heal so you can move and the added risk of spending longer in the badlands. Of course, there may be no choice if you cannot walk. Given medical equipment, food and a suitably remote bit of country you can make a camping holiday out of it while your wounds heal but far more likely is that you will be in constant fear of discovery by locals and shortage of water or food. So probably you will have to press on as soon as you can walk.

## WHAT SURVIVAL EQUIPMENT DO
## I HAVE WITH ME?

We will look at survival equipment later but the more equipment you have with you, the more comfortable you are going to be and the less risks you will have to take. Wouldn't it be nice to have a radio or electronic beacon to call a flying taxi and a sheet which makes you invisible to infrared viewers? And nice warm clothing and...

If you can purify water or have concentrated rations, you don't have to take the risk of stealing. These do not weigh much as so should be carried where this is practical. Medical equipment such as antibiotics, sutures (stitches) and painkillers don't weigh much either. If you have weapons or explosives, you can make following you a more interesting occupation. If you have hunting or fishing equipment, in many places you can survive indefinitely as long as you have a taste for raw meat.

## WHAT IS THE BEST ROUTE?

You really ought to have a good idea where in the world you are and what the country and climate are like. If you have any sense at all, you will have a map. Weighing up who is chasing you, how much trouble they might go to, how populated the countryside is and what roads, traffic, rivers, railways and so on there are leading in the direction you are travelling will give you an idea of how to set about covering the ground to get where you need to be.

Of course, this might be an agreed RV with a helicopter or it might be 320 km (200 miles) to get out of foreign airspace before the taxi will take your call. It might be a walk to the coast to steal a boat or if you are important enough your boss might send a submarine to collect you off the coast.

When you know where you have to get to, what the country is like, what condition you are in and who is looking for you, then you are well placed to make an estimate of how long it will take. And therefore how long you are going to have to keep warm or cool, drink and eat and walk.

This is where you are glad you brought the water-sterilisation pills, survival rations, compass and radio. Or not.

## CAN I STEAL TRANSPORT?

Even when you know how to do it, and you will if you keep reading, there is always a risk to stealing transport. The first choice is to do the tab on foot if you can. Of course, you can walk hundreds of miles if you want, but there comes a point where the journey is so long that time spent walking increases the risk so much that a lift of some kind is worth trying for.

Trains are easy to get on but difficult to hide in and always searched in these situations. Cars usually have to travel on roads which are easy to block and search but they are quick. Depending on the country, you could go for four-footed transport but it is hardly worth the risk for the small speed advantage. A camel plods on at four clicks an hour, uphill and down. Walking, you should be able to cover 100km (60 miles) in two days without breaking sweat. If you can't do that, you have no business being a soldier. A car or truck can do this distance in less than an hour without draining you at all. Look at the time-at-risk you are avoiding.

## CAN I STEAL FOOD?

If there are people about you can always steal food but again it may well not be worth the risk. And if you are only going to be on the run a day or two, forget it. You do not need to eat for four days unless you are very weak. You will, however, need water by the second day to keep going.

## WHAT IS THE POSITION OF THE LOCAL POPULATION?

The local people will almost certainly be against you. Why otherwise would you be there? Even if they are not, it only takes one of the family or neighbours to inform on you for a reward. Assume the locals are against you and plan to avoid them as best you can. We'll consider this further later.

## DO I WANT TO RAISE THE STAKES?

If you are running from a fire-fight the people chasing you are going to kill you if they catch you. But, if you have escaped from prison, a hostage situation or a fight in a bar, then, as long as you have not killed anyone, your pursuers may not kill you on the spot, or even later.

You now need to decide how far you are prepared to raise the stakes. If you kill people in an attempt to stay free, it may keep you free and get you home. On the other hand, if you are later caught, it might mean you are hanged. I suggest you try not to hurt innocent civilians in any event and keep away from your pursuers rather than confront them where this is possible. But, as I said earlier, if you have to fight, fight hard.

## AM I BEING PURSUED BY MILITIA, TERRORISTS OR GOVERNMENT FORCES?

If the local militia or army has shot down your chopper or wasted your mates, they are going to be coming for you in hot pursuit. They will be chasing rather than tracking or searching. We have already seen how to break off a contact or flee the scene of an aircraft wreck, so now we need to look at what happens next. I don't want to see you on an internet video having your head hacked off with a carving knife, so listen up. The chances are that people you have just been fighting will be quite keen to catch you until they lose your trail and at this point they will probably give up or pass the word to locals friendly to them that you are in the area.

On the other hand, if you have broken out of a prison of some kind or escaped arrest or a fight in a bar, there may well be government forces searching for you. This means police or military and if you are important enough – meaning you have done something serious enough – government forces across the whole area or country may be alerted and stay on the job indefinitely. This can mean searches of likely ground, villages, trains and road vehicles. So if there were not already checkpoints on the main roads and some streets there may be now. Your smiling face may be in the newspapers and TV so the locals know what you look like. And, even if we all look the same to them, you may well be the only European or North American in the area, so you will be lifted on sight.

The effort government agencies make to catch you, of course, might range from an existing checkpoint pulling you if they remember the picture of the guy who glassed a couple of locals in a bar to a whole range of efforts if you are a successful spy. The only ways to catch you once you are out of sight of the people you escaped from is by tracking you down along your path, searching the likely areas you might have to cross or setting up roadblocks and checkpoints. We will look at tracking and searching now; then roadblocks and checkpoints in the next chapter as they are an art in themselves and you would do well to understand them.

## DIRECT PURSUIT – TRACKING

Given you are out in the sticks and your pursuers know where you started from, they can track you along your own path by either scent with a dog or by tracking with a human. If your pursuers are Muslims, they may be reluctant to use dogs on religious grounds, but don't count on it.

If there are dogs on your trail, there are only two ways to get away that I know of because dogs and their handlers can follow you at the run. Either you set up a series of explosive booby-traps to slow them right down, as I explained earlier, or you steal a motor vehicle and outrun them. Anything you may have heard about crossing water or taking to the trees to lose dogs is bullshit. Many dogs can track across water and after rain, but if you do cross a river or other water all they do is take one dog one way and another dog the other way until they catch your scent again. Dogs are brilliant for chasing men down but less good if you are the quarry. A lady I know trains them for the British Police and you would be amazed at what they can do when properly trained.

It always seems strange to me that you only find trackers out in the wilds. Anyone with reasonable eyesight can learn the basics of tracking in a day and become moderately good by practising over a few weeks. Anyone can follow footprints in mud but tracking is really just an extension of looking for the marks made by someone passing that way. After a while, you get to see the changes in the way the light reflects off grass, bushes and soil when it has been brushed against by someone passing by. Still, there it is. The chances of a decent tracker coming after you in Europe are pretty remote. In Africa, watch out!

I once worked with a tracker who was so good he could follow a man walking across featureless terrain at terrific speed. I need to look at prints and rocks and bushes but this old guy used to sit on the front of an armoured car and guide it at driving speed across country after the quarry. Mind you, by the look of him, he had probably been tracking critters for 80 years.

The best way to avoid capture when someone is tracking you is to move faster than them, but this is not always possible. Given you can't outrun them, you need to slow them down. As we have seen, you can do this by confusing them or making them wary. Probably the best way to slow the pursuit is to make them cautious. There are two main ways to do this: booby-traps and ambush.

You can rig an effective booby-trap by loosening the pin in a grenade and tying it to a tree. Run a cord from the grenade pin across the track and tie it to another tree or rock. It only takes a moment, but when the pursuit comes they are likely to pull the pin and give themselves a fright. This will make even the most religious watch their step and move slowly while you are running like hell.

A more primitive delaying technique depends on the right terrain, bushes and your having time to set it up. Cut a few stakes at least 10cm (4 inches) long and make a small hole in the pathway. Set the stakes point up in the bottom and cover the hole with leaves or branches. When the pursuers arrive, one is likely to step on the leaves and will drop with some force, impaling their foot on the spikes. (These could be covered with excrement for disgust and disease value.) This will only wound one person but it will make the others walk more carefully and possibly have to carry their mate.

Ambushing your pursuers is very easy to set up and massively satisfying as long as there are not too many of them. Here the old 'dog-leg' never fails. Turn off your path and double back to a place where, if possible, the ground overlooks the path you have come along. Those following you will be coming along the same track and so you will be able to shoot or grenade the first man or commander. Shoot during the day but at night use a grenade if you can as this will not give away your position. The idea of the high or broken ground is to make it hard for the people you are ambushing to come at you. When you are in a group trying to avoid being ambushed, you spread out lengthways, so watch out for the people you are ambushing doing the same thing. The last thing you want to do is hit a little advance party and tell all their mates where you are.

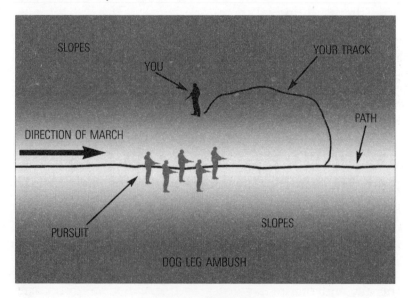

## SEARCH PARTIES

If you are worth the trouble, someone on the other side who wants to see your pretty face will start searching for you. Hopefully, you will be long gone but if you are waiting for an extraction or 'lying up' during the day this could be a problem.

Clearly they know where you started from and how far you might have travelled on foot. They may well know which way you have to go, so it may not be rocket science to narrow down where you might be to an area worth searching.

In villages or towns, any locals who are suspected collaborators will have their houses searched and everyone will have their outbuildings searched. You cannot be sure they will not use dogs and if they do they will find you. This would be very bad. Out in the sticks they will look everywhere in the area you could be in which is likely to provide shelter and, again, if they use dogs they will find you.

The best thing you can do about search parties when you are lying up is not be there. If you have to stop there are ways to improve your situation. The best of these is to be hidden by a friendly local, but it is a lucky man who knows who his friends are.

If you have to stop and do not have someone to hide you, lie up well away from any buildings, roads and prominent features like bridges and caves. This avoids giving the searchers a reason to look where you are and means they will only get you by combing every inch of the ground.

Depending on the situation, there may be a search from the air, and the effectiveness of this will depend on the technical abilities of the people looking, the type of country and the size of the area you might be found in. If the country is covered in bush or forest, aircraft are a waste of time and you only have to fear a ground search.

If the ground is open and sparsely covered you need to be careful.

During daylight a great deal can be seen from the air, as you may know, but unless the target is wearing a prisoner's orange outfit or similar it is remarkably difficult to pick out individuals from a great height even over flat, open ground. If there are aircraft looking for you over a large area you just need to keep still and out of sight when they pass over. High-level spotting of people takes very special kit and time to analyse the results – by which time you will have moved on.

If the searchers have aircraft with infrared, the only way to not be detected at night, by the heat signature you give off, is to cover yourself with either earth or a specially treated sheet which blocks your heat signature. This is a lot of trouble to go to so it is best to know what the opposition have. What will make things easier for you, however, is that there may well be other people travelling in the area, herdsmen and suchlike, in which case the infrared searchers will have to check everyone if they are only picking up traces of bodies. So you only need to worry about infrared if the opposition have the kit and you are in an open, uninhabited area.

When you are working out your route, you should weigh the benefits of having close cover to hide in against the extra time to get through it and the detour you might have to make to take advantage of it.

When you have considered all the points above to the best of your ability you will be able to make a plan to give you the best chance of getting home. In the real world there will be a lot fewer questions to work through as you consider your options. Here I am giving you an aide-memoire to teach you to handle any situation, whereas when it happens to you for real most of the answers will be obvious. While you are putting this plan into operation, you can think about losing the pursuit.

# Chapter Seven

# Stealing Transport

Your choice of transport is usually going to be a trade-off between speed, comfort and less time spent in the area against the risk of being caught taking the ride. If you have more than a few clicks to cover, riding in or on something is clearly preferable to walking. As I said earlier, a vehicle will allow you to cover in an hour what would take two days on foot. If you or someone in your team is injured and struggling to walk, hitching a ride might make all the difference to your survival. One way or the other.

The problem is that, if you take someone's transport, they are going to miss it when they next need it and they will tell whoever is looking for you. If you take a vehicle while someone is in it, when you have finished with the ride you either have to let them go or make a hard decision. You are also more likely to be spotted travelling by road. Read what I have to say about the subject and then use your wits according to the situation you find yourself in.

## BEFORE YOU GET INTO TROUBLE, LEARN TO DRIVE ANYTHING

Before you go into harm's way you should learn to drive any form of transport you are likely to come across. You do not need to go so far as to get yourself a licence, you just need to be able to start it up and guide it. That means you should be able to drive a car with either manual or automatic transmission and have had a go in a truck to get the feel of it.

You should learn to ride a motorcycle, which are all much the same, as they are extremely handy for cross-country use, on rough tracks and in city-centre pedestrian areas.

You should take sailing lessons in a dinghy of some kind. If you can sail a dinghy, you can sail a larger boat after a fashion and that is good enough.

Motor boats are point and steer if you can get the engine going, so a working knowledge of diesel engines is no bad thing either, as you can be sure you will have a breakdown or the boat you steal will not start easily.

I rather like horses and camels as they are quiet and go a long way on one tank of gas, but I know some men have issues. Get over it and learn how to ride them.

### RIDING TRAINS

Before we look at driving something yourself, let's briefly consider trains. These are a mixed blessing when it comes to escaping. On the good side, they are easy to find and board, as you just look for the tracks and wait where they have to slow down for a bend or station; and they travel in a straight line between all the places of interest for sometimes thousands of miles.

The trouble is that the people looking for you know

this too and trains are the first place they will search if they think you are going that way. Ticket inspectors patrol the carriages of passenger trains and clearly you won't have a ticket and you will look suspicious if you are on a wanted poster or do not speak the language. If you can get a ticket and speak the language, all you have to worry about is being recognised and extra searches by the security forces if they are on your trail.

Don't try to hide under a train in a station, as on the old types of train where this is possible it is the first place they will look. You might be lucky with a goods train if you can get well hidden among the load and perhaps it is raining or dark so the searchers become sloppy.

The best way to use trains is to get on a goods train after it has left the station and been searched and get off before it stops at the next station. I know this can be tricky as you may not know where it is going to stop, but if you know the lie of the land it may be obvious that a train which is full of coal, for example, is going all the way to the docks on the coast. It is not likely to stop for the coal to stretch its legs but it may for a crew change.

If you have to get off because the train is approaching a city or a smaller station where it is likely to be searched, make sure you move around the city or the station in a wide enough circle to avoid roadblocks and other dangers. But don't forget that the people looking for a stowaway may be expecting this avoidance procedure.

## TAKING ANIMALS

You should be able to ride a horse or camel if you might come across them while on a mission. More than that, you need to be able to saddle them up and at least handle the basics of maintaining them for a few days. What this means in practice, after you have put a bridle and saddle on the animal, is hobbling it at night and knowing how much food and water to get into it to keep it going.

With horses you need to know how to get them to stand still while you get on and then how to make them go forward, left, right and stop. If you can change gait – from a walk to a trot to a canter – so much the better. All horses kick and bite, so watch out for both ends.

Camels only really have one gear so, if you can get them to lie down while you get on and then, more difficult, stay on while they stand up, you are away. Camels are known for being nasty because they are treated so badly in the parts of the world where they are common. A well-handled camel is actually a really nice creature to deal with. The other sort will bite and spit without hesitation. I mentioned earlier a mate of mine who took camel trains into Afghanistan carrying missiles from the CIA to the Taliban and he told me some horrific stories about the sort of camels they have there. Did you know that if a camel bites you there is a 100 per cent chance of getting an infection and the bitten limb dropping off?

Learning beforehand to ride a horse or a camel is a lot of effort for something you are not likely to use, so most men are not keen, but make your own decision.

For travelling quickly, riding an animal is not much use at all. Most are slow and stubborn and no competition on the road for any sort of motor. Where they come into their own is just the odd occasion on certain types of rough or soft country where walking is hard work across marsh, desert or mountainside and you are not likely to be spotted. In cases like this, you just might be glad you learned how to drive one.

## TAKING A MOTOR VEHICLE

I will say again that taking a motor vehicle of any kind is raising the stakes a great deal. You are going to potentially move fast and leave pursuers behind, cutting down your time in enemy territory, but you are also taking the extra risk of being caught either stealing the motor or at a checkpoint on the road. This risk has to be weighed against the risk of walking or whatever. You may also hurt someone during the exercise and if you are caught this might make your situation worse, if that is possible.

There are two ways to get yourself a car, truck or motorcycle. You can either take one from where it has been left parked or you can take one while someone is using it. Both of these strategies have advantages and disadvantages, as you will see.

If you are going to take a motor from its garage or parking spot, you need to be able to start the engine and get the steering lock off. This is a little more complicated than it may seem with modern cars but old ones with no steering lock are easy. All you need to do is connect the ignition wire under the dash and touch the solenoid wires together for a moment to turn the starter motor.

I won't tell you here how to take modern cars as I don't want to encourage the wrong sort of person, so I suggest you get a bunch of lads together and ask your commanding officer to set up a course for you. The boss can soon get in someone from the police who knows how it is done.

The idea is to take a car when you know someone is not going to want it for a while and in most places that is going to be last thing at night. It is worth staking out a suitable house and waiting for them to go to bed. Some criminals in Europe rob houses to get the vehicle's keys but I would not normally recommend that as it increases risk for a low chance of getting them. Unless of course you are prepared to kill the occupants of the house. All of them. I would rather not.

When someone in a Western had to keep another person in one place and stop them warning the sheriff, he just tied them up, safe in the knowledge they would be found the next day after he was well clear of the area. If you do this, be aware you may be sentencing the people you tie up to a long, slow death by dehydration if they are not found.

If the car is missed, the police will be informed and in most situations they will have a good idea who has taken it and be on to you like a shot.

A safer way to get a motor is actually to take it while it is in use as they do in many African cities and recently some in Europe. Do not try to stop a car by lying down in the road on a quiet bend as the driver will, if he doesn't go around you, run you over.

What you need to do is pick a suitable spot which is quiet but where motors are parked. Select your vehicle of choice, and it will have to be four-wheeled for obvious reasons, then wait quietly for the owner to return. As they approach their car, mind elsewhere, make your move and stand in front of them pointing your pistol into their face. If you have no gun, use a knife but it must be pushed up against their throat while you hold them.

I suggest you pick a man rather than a woman as a

woman is more likely to turn hysterical and lose the plot. This would just make her unmanageable and ruin the operation. With a man, you need to be sufficiently intimidating to let him know you mean business but move slowly enough for him to catch on to what is happening. Think about it, if someone came up to you while your mind was elsewhere, wouldn't it take you a moment or two to understand what was wanted? Especially if the person only spoke 'foreign'. Look him in the eye, pointing the gun in his face for a moment, then nod towards the driving seat. It should be plain what is required.

Once in the car, hold the gun to his ribs the whole time in case he gets an attack of bravery. Most men will do as they are told in this situation and not even try to call for help or take the gun off you. Be ready for this, though. You can easily point out directions with your free hand and make good progress for some hours if necessary.

Things do get tricky if you come across a roadblock. To turn around and get away you need to be able to see it far enough ahead. While this often happens at roadblocks because people don't want to queue, it can look suspicious and the men on the roadblock may come after you. Sorry, I don't have all the answers here.

What you should be doing really is taking a vehicle only when you can have some confidence there will not be a roadblock because you are moving too fast, the opposition are not sufficiently organised or you are not important enough. If you do end up in a roadblock, just hope to God it is not organised properly, then you may get away with luck and a following wind. For more on this, see the next chapter.

The sticky bit is leaving the vehicle and its owner. If you are collected by others, or are back on the safe side of the border, there is little problem, but, if you are intending to continue on foot because the road doesn't go the right way or the car has broken down, you are stuck with a prisoner you cannot guard or feed for very long. If you let him go, he will tell the authorities as fast as he can. If you take him with you, you'll have to watch him. The hard answer is to kill him but call me a softie if you like: I am not comfortable with that. Perhaps it is best to walk him some distance and tie him up and gag him. That is certainly better than the alternative from his point of view.

## TAKING A BOAT

Should you come across one on your travels, a boat will have a whole load of advantages over walking. It is much easier to take a boat than a car without anyone knowing about it. They are easier to start and often very quiet. A motor boat or sailing boat less than 12 metres (40 feet) long is easier to operate alone. The engine room will not be separate from the driving position, the controls will be easy to work out and there will not be too many masts and sails for one person to handle.

Motor boats are better than sailing boats on rivers and enclosed waterways as they go where you point them at a speed suitable to the area. That is why you found it there. The only problems are starting the engine and running out of fuel.

The bigger the boat the more distance it should be capable of covering, but what you can find will be a matter of luck. An inboard engine, usually a diesel, will probably have a large fuel tank while an outboard may not be so generous with fuel and therefore range. And outboards are thirsty and noisy compared with a plodding diesel.

An outboard may start with just the pull of a cord or a key may be involved and this will be tricky. Just pick something you can start and if it is too close to the neighbours paddle away first. An inboard diesel should start with a handle or cord unless it is on the larger side, in which case it may be a battery start. Rarely is a key required.

You will probably get away with starting and steering a motor boat even if you have never been on one before but a sailing boat is a different kettle of fish entirely. There is a knack to steering and trimming the sails to make the thing move through the water and stay upright which has to be learned. It is not hard to do well enough for our needs but you do need to be shown. Sailing boats are relatively slow and obviously move in the general direction of the wind, so to move against the wind you have to steer a zigzag course called tacking. Go to a sailing club to learn more. This is good fun, even sober.

The important and wonderful thing about sailing boats is that they do not run out of fuel. If you can get on to open water, even in a small dinghy you can sail indefinitely in the general direction of home.

When it comes to crossing a river, particularly if the weather is cold and no bridge is in sight, a boat is infinitely preferable to swimming across as the cold water alone can kill you or at least sap a lot of your energy. Cut the boat adrift when you have crossed so that it is not clear to the opposition whether you have just crossed or gone upstream or down. This can buy a little time. That said, on any river at night or on a big river even through a town, there is a big advantage in gliding downstream – as long as there are no patrols looking for you. If you take a small motor boat at night you have at least 12 hours or so to cover some ground, or in this case water. This could easily be 80–95km (50–60 miles) as you have the speed of the current on top of whatever speed you make through the water with oars or motor. And the wonderful thing about rivers is that they pretty much all go to the sea.

## TAKING AN AIRCRAFT

I can fly an autogiro, a microlight, a small helicopter or a single-engined plane but I wouldn't try my luck with anything like a military chopper or a multi-engined fixed-wing aircraft. It would be quicker to walk than to figure out the controls.

Unless you have a passion for it, and can already fly something, you are not going to become proficient on any sort of useful aircraft. On top of this, every aircraft is fairly complicated and different from every other. The chances of coming across one you are familiar with are not worth considering.

The good news is that there is little chance of your stealing a flying machine anyway as most airfields are much more closely guarded than you might think from watching *Mission: Impossible*.

On the other hand, a ride in a plane is the answer to all your prayers as it will get you home, or at least away from the bad guys, in short order. So how do you hitch a ride?

I am afraid this is neither easy nor safe but if the

occasion arises it can be done. It just takes a lot of nerve and a lot more bluff. You have to get yourself in a plane with, hopefully, just the pilot and enough fuel on board to get you home.

The best way to do this is to find yourself an airfield which is not too well guarded. OK, in some countries such a thing just doesn't exist and the only airfields are military, but in some countries there are crop sprayers operating out of barns and private airfields for sport or taxi flying. Find one if you can.

When a plane is out on the apron, the area around the runway, it is always under the eye of the control tower unless it is an extremely small airfield. This is a bad time to approach it as you will be seen to be up to no good and there are other planes to chase you. At the very least the tower can call the military. And their planes *will* catch you.

A small civilian airfield or private strip will be easiest and therefore safest, so choose this if there is a choice. You should be so lucky. Find yourself a plane which is out of the way in a hangar or barn. It should not be too big as you don't want many passengers. Hide in the plane if there is room to hide, but it's better to hide nearby if possible. This is because before a pilot takes up a plane of any kind he should do pre-flight checks, steering, breaks instruments and suchlike, and he may well have to get fuel from a bowser or other supply. It is better in many ways to be watching all this done from the outside from the point of view of knowing what is happening and timing your move. If he does not do his pre-flight checks carefully you might want to reconsider hitching a ride with him.

When you judge the time to be right, the plane is fuelled, if possible, and no passengers are coming, step out and point your pistol at his face. This generally gets the message across in most languages. As I have said elsewhere, pilots are not known for their stupidity, so he ought to catch on to your plan. Put finger to lips to tell him to be quiet and encourage him to board the aircraft. See if he will admit to speaking English as most flyers are educated and the international language of the air is English. If he does, tell him that you will shoot him if he warns the control tower or otherwise disobeys you. Tell him you are heading north, or whatever, for X hundred miles. Watch his face for clues as to the possibility of achieving this. Watch out for tricks as pilots also have nerve and will trick you if they can.

Explain that you will be killed if caught and therefore have nothing to lose. Get both of you in the plane and have him take off. Even if he has to speak to the tower, make him think you know enough of the local language to tell if he is warning anyone. Have him take off, then change the order for direction to what you really want just in case he got a brief message to the tower.

Make him fly at less than 150 metres (500 feet) to keep under commercial radar and make the plane harder to see from a distance. A single-engined plane ought to cruise at no less than 130 knots (150mph/240kmph) so it will not take too long to get somewhere. Keep your eyes on the altimeter, the compass and the airspeed indicator and you will always have a good idea of your general position. For example, one hour at 130 knots travelling East gets me to…

If he shows signs of trickery, make him aware that you

know enough to bring the plane down alone. As I said, you should be able to put the fear of death into a pilot to win his cooperation. Look upon this as getting your own back for all the fear pilots have given you over the years.

Once in the air, you might think it odd to consider the idea of shooting the pilot. He might think the same. But if he is flying the wrong way you either do something or get caught. Remember you can always shoot or cut bits off him if there is a conflict of wills and that it is much easier to guide a plane to where you want to be or put one on the ground than take off in the first place. After all, you have gravity on your side.

Whatever the pilot might say, a small plane will put down on grass. It may not get off the ground again under its own steam, but it will land in one piece.

The chances are that road transport is what you are going to end up with. You can steal it, you can drive it and it is freely available. Now how do you avoid the roadblocks?

## Chapter Eight

# Roadblocks And Checkpoints

It's pretty obvious, and you have probably operated them yourself, but I am going to remind you that the purpose of static roadblocks and checkpoints is to stop people and things being moved from one place to another. Very often this means stopping terrorist forces regrouping or sending supplies one to another. In the present case, it means stopping you moving any great distance on a road or into or out of a town. Movable checkpoints, on the other hand, are for catching people.

As a rule checkpoints are for checking people. They mark the position where pedestrians are stopped and potentially searched. These may be asked for ID and are certainly checked as to what language they speak and if they really should have blonde hair, blue eyes and be carrying a pistol. You find most checkpoints guard the entrance to places of interest such as civic buildings, which is of little concern to you, and to towns, which might be. This is more to protect the buildings and people inside than to catch people. These checkpoints act as a deterrent because, in principle, the bad guys know they are there and don't go.

A good example of the use of checkpoints is the 'ring of steel' around Belfast. Some years ago, a tall, spiky security fence several miles long ran all around the centre of the city and set in it were pedestrian checkpoints where the locals were searched at random for bombs, weapons and so on. The idea was to stop weapons and bombs coming into the city centre. As well as being an excellent place for meeting the local girls, it was fairly effective at its job. For this reason you are advised not to try to go into a major city or town where there is a military presence of this kind. A sort of add-on to checkpoints is the random stop-and-search you may well come across in any place where you are on the run. So keep away from towns if you can.

Static roadblocks are merely the vehicle equivalent of checkpoints. Vehicles can carry a great deal more contraband a lot further than people, so they are used for this purpose whenever possible. Everything from smuggling bombs and fighters to moving untaxed vodka. Then there are random, movable roadblocks and these are a pain. The trouble is, of course, that you don't know where they are going to be. While there are always vehicle checks on the entry roads to at-risk towns, a great many roadblocks are set up at random along busy roads. This is useful to those searching because it is much more difficult to turn around from a roadblock in a car or truck than from a checkpoint when on foot. Anyone who does turn their vehicle around will be checked or shot, depending on the circumstances.

One rainy night we were setting up the endless mobile

roadblocks then used in the countryside of Northern Ireland. We were wet and bored, far too sober, and wanted to be somewhere else. The roadblock was set up pretty well, with two Land Rovers staggered on opposite sides of the road in a fashion which slowed traffic right down. Also we had front and back cover out – guards or 'stops' a few yards either way along from the road from the roadblock – and the roadblock itself was on a bend, out of sight of approaching traffic until the last moment.

Before anyone knew what was happening, a yellow sports saloon had come around the corner, seen us, done a handbrake turn and set off away from us. Our rules of engagement did not allow us to fire into any vehicle that was not endangering the patrol and the 'stop' was too slow getting the tyre-ripping chain across the road, so we had to let them go. It was obvious someone had their wits about them and could drive like a demon.

Clearly, you want to avoid towns and their static checkpoints but you may well want to increase your speed of movement by stealing a vehicle and taking it along a road which may be infested with static roadblocks or may be a likely target for random roadblocks.

## STATIC PEDESTRIAN CHECKPOINT

This is a gate or similar manned by several bored guards who may be police, army or from some sort of private security firm. As I said, static pedestrian checkpoints are placed around town centres when traffic is banned within these areas to protect buildings, and alongside vehicle checkpoints at borders.

The town centres should be no problem once you are out of town as you won't go back into a town again.

Protected buildings the same. The only place a pedestrian checkpoint should be a problem is if you need to cross a border. All I can say about this is that you don't cross a border at the checkpoint. No matter you are in a vehicle or on foot, you leave the road and cross somewhere quiet. Obvious, I know, but some smart-arse might try disguising themselves in a burka.

## MOVABLE PEDESTRIAN CHECKPOINT

A mobile pedestrian checkpoint is called stop-and-search. At times of heightened security concerns, such as when there has been a terrorist attack or when they may be looking for you, there may be a policy in town to search all the Europeans or whatever you are. If you stand out by reason of skin colour, dress or other signs, some keen officer is just bound to come over to talk to you, even if it is only to take a few smokes off you. It is a good idea always to carry a packet of cigarettes in prisons and countries where the police take bribes as it smoothes your path no end. If you slip a cigarette to the con dishing out the uniforms in a prison, you will get a better outfit and be marked as someone they can deal with in their little economy. If you slip a copper a cigarette, or a banknote in your passport, it may make the difference between being hauled in just to give them something to do and being given directions with a salute.

## STATIC ROADBLOCK CHECKPOINT

Again, static roadblocks are a form of deterrent; this time designed to stop the bad guys (bad from the roadblock operator's point of view) moving heavy loads or people any real distance conveniently. All the locals will know where the roadblocks are – around the city and government buildings, and on certain highways – and avoid them when they can. You should do the same. When approaching a static roadblock on the main road, you will just have to leave your transport as you will not get through without a shooting match.

## MOBILE ROADBLOCK CHECKPOINT

When you are travelling by road across country in a motor, mobile roadblocks are the big problem. If the government, or the warlord running the area, is looking for you, there is likely to be mobile roadblocks along your intended route. They are very difficult to avoid when set up properly and form the main argument against travelling by road.

This is how a mobile roadblock should be set up in a perfect world.

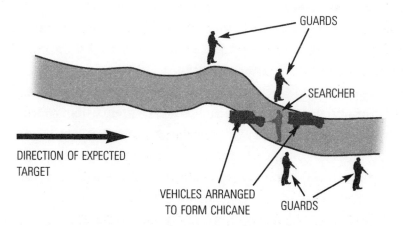

GUARDS

SEARCHER

DIRECTION OF EXPECTED TARGET

VEHICLES ARRANGED TO FORM CHICANE

GUARDS

What you are up against may be this or something less efficient, according to the situation and the people doing the blocking. You will see that the vehicles are arranged to make the traffic slow right down. There are guards covering the searcher from a safe distance and there are 'stops' at the front and rear of the roadblock both to protect it and to stop anyone getting away.

The perfect way to avoid roadblocks is not open to you. This is to have a car in front with good papers and squeaky clean in every way. It drives half a mile or so ahead of you and radios back if it comes across a roadblock. Then it goes through itself. The chances of a roadblock being set up between the two cars is so remote as to make this system very safe. Sadly, you are unlikely to be able to take advantage of this trick as you are alone, have no papers and are probably holding the driver at gunpoint.

You can very slightly lessen your chances of being stopped by looking boring by being in an ordinary vehicle, driving steadily and having no one inside who looks interesting. But a properly set roadblock should check them all or pick cars at random to avoid just this ploy.

Also, you can drive slowly and where the road ahead is hidden you might sometimes stop the car and do a recce ahead on foot, but this is tedious.

If you are stopped, there are only two things you can do: either put the driver in such fear of his life that he does not give you away on the grounds of expecting instant death at your hands, or start shooting.

Your chances of success when trying to sneak through like this vary widely according to the country and situation. If the locals don't carry papers and look like you, you just might get away with it. Avoid the eyes of the man checking the papers as this may give him a clue you are not a sheep. If he moves suddenly you might be as well killing him and trying to drive through.

My preference would be to get out of the car as if injured or infirm and try to get close to the guards before starting the shooting yourself. If there are only a handful and they are not spread out properly as shown above, you have a good chance of survival and of collecting better weapons, ammunition, cigarettes and even water and food. Remember, get them close, take the movers first, then the others. Don't get excited, and kill them all quickly. If you are on a quiet stretch of road, it might even be worth your while rolling the bodies into the bushes and hiding the vehicles to gain a few hours. Before you get out to try this, you might want to take the ignition keys in case the driver gets any ideas.

Then get moving.

My introduction to this sort of road work came courtesy of the British Army in Wales. The course I was on was designed, among other things, to cover defensive driving for taking care of VIPs and similar targets. This involved knowing how to play both the hound and the hare.

We were formed into teams of three, each team with a police driving instructor, possibly not a usual instructor, and set off across Wales with a free pass against speeding tickets and other motoring offences. It was about the most fun you can have without lying down.

Among other penalties, we were fined a hefty contribution to the end-of-course beer fund for parking face-in as this makes for a slow getaway. To this day I never park face-in even in a supermarket. We were taught the 'J' turn, which looks quite flash but is actually pretty simple to do. All you have to do is drive quickly enough so the tyres will come unstuck from the road, flick the steering to the right, then touch the footbrake pedal gently to slow the front wheels. As you do this, jam the handbrake on hard so the back wheels lock up and the back end of the car slides around to the left. While it is turning, put the clutch in, straighten the steering as the car faces the right way, go into first gear and let out the clutch as you hit the gas and take off the handbrake. All it takes is a little practice in a quiet spot.

Another little driving trick which can come in handy when you are under pressure is the 'block change'. This means changing gear from, say, fourth to second or from third to first. The purpose is to get away quickly by keeping the engine revving high as you pull away from a tight corner or bend. Suppose you are coming in fast to a short, tight bend. In order not to lose time, you might want to slide the back end out to turn the car to face the way out of the bend. Also, you will be approaching the bend in top gear and want to break hard and late but be able to accelerate hard out of the bend. To do this you pick your moment while you are at the end of the braking run and about to cut into the bend proper, then you put the clutch in, gun the engine to bring the revs up to match the low gear, then select the correct gear for coming out of the bend. This might be first or it might be second. Easier to do than say.

# Chapter Nine

# Treatment Of Civilians

You'll need to know how to befriend, capture, kill or avoid civilians – and when to do each. The rule you should live by when working abroad as a soldier is that you don't go to any trouble to antagonise the locals. There is no advantage. The problem is that the very fact you are there may make them hate you. Imagine if their army were strutting about your town and searching you and your girlfriend when they felt like it. Worse, breaking into your house in the dead of night and lining everyone up against a wall while they search the place. Then they take your dad away and torture him... Even the British arrest people in this way and, although they don't use torture, those arrested will say they did, which can stir up just as much trouble.

Wherever you are, you will have a good idea of what the locals think about you. If you are an occupying force, they will hate you. If you are holding back the terrorists, maybe they will love you or maybe they support the opposition.

Civilians are not stupid, although soldiers sometimes think they are. What they are doing is trying to make the best of their situation. If they hate you, they most likely can't show it much or you would arrest them. If they love you, they may have to be careful or their neighbour will tip off the bad guys, who will shoot them as collaborators. Civilians have the worst hand in every conflict.

Unless they are mob-handed, locals almost everywhere will pretend to love the occupying forces. If you are on your own and far from home, they may act a little differently. Especially as there may be a reward from the opposition for information about fugitives. Or for your weapons or ears.

Not only that but there is a good chance you won't even be able to communicate with them. Do you speak the lingo of the last place you were posted? I have never managed to pick up more than a smattering of half a dozen languages as I find languages difficult and have never been in one place long enough. The chances are it will be the same for you. Places that speak your language will generally not be at war with you and, while the educated elite in most countries speak English, the people you meet out in the sticks will almost certainly not.

When you are on patrol, showing the flag in town, you don't want to let them get too near you. Even if 99 out of 100 think you are the best thing since sliced bread, the one that hates you, whose mum the last team in the area killed while shooting at the bad guys, will be coming to get you. And will look just the same as everyone else on the street. Except she will have a bomb under the dead baby on her back.

So smile and try to look friendly, just like they do, but keep your eyes open for the one who wants to kill you. On a long posting, when all is quiet, staying alert like this takes real determination. By contrast, keeping your eye on the ball is easy when something kicks off in town and there is a riot or a crowd gathers after a bomb has taken out your lead vehicle. The general principle to stick to is: don't make contact with the locals unless you absolutely have to or you are in a situation where you are sure they will give you support against the opposition. This can be a little more often than you might suppose, given the way that the opposition in many places use the locals as a supply of food and women.

If the opposition is in hot pursuit, it doesn't matter a damn if some little goatherd sees you, but if you are passing silently through the countryside you may have to kill him or her. Best make it look like an accident with a blow to the front of the head. Better still, don't get yourself into this unpleasant situation. Avoid the locals like the plague and keep an eye out for farming and livestock.

What I would call a definite need to contact the locals is if you are so wounded you cannot travel or if you are starving. In either case, where there is a fair chance of a friendly reception you might give it a try. At this point you will wish you had learned the language a whole lot better and given some thought to the local customs. That said, if they are with you they will help you and if they aren't they won't, whatever you say or do.

## How Governments Use Civilians

I know the following is not exactly on message but I am going to tell you a few things about how governments use civilians, so that when the civilians start showing off you might feel a bit more sympathy towards them.

In the modern age the media report everything and public

opinion does matter. They cover things with a slant which suits the owner of the newspaper, TV channel or radio station, and he has friends in politics. But events are still events and it matters, even to the harshest despot, that his actions should appear plausible to people in his own and particularly other countries. He will do this so that his own followers will continue to support him and democratic countries cannot muster a universal UN vote to impose sanctions against him or go to war or whatever.

In Gaza, the terrorists fire at least 30 rockets at Israeli civilians every day and it hardly makes the news, but as soon as the Israelis try to stop them the world media condemn them. Then there is Zimbabwe, where the dictator Robert Mugabe, may he rot in Hell, controls the local media and bans the BBC as he starves and murders his own people.

The following are tricks which governments have used and are still using to make life hell for civilians they want to control.

### ETHNIC CLEANSING – DARFUR

Sudan is in North Africa and is Africa's largest country. Darfur, itself the size of France, is a province in the west of Sudan which abuts Chad and the Central African Republic. In Darfur, most of the people are African, dark-skinned farmers who try to make a living out of the harsh, dry land. The rest of Sudan is populated by Arabs who are herders of goats, camels and suchlike. There was originally something of a competition for land and water and the politicians, all Arab, decided it was in their interest to support their fellow Arabs irrespective of right or wrong. The plan was that by driving out the Africans, the Arabs would gain their land. Nothing new there then.

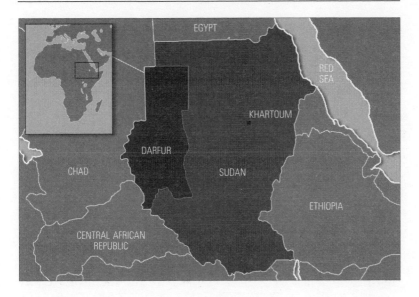

This plot began with the government using aircraft to bomb the Africans but when this became too much of a problem on the international stage they changed tactics and secretly allowed local Arab bandits to launch raids into Darfur, burning, raping and killing on a massive scale. Despite almost worldwide condemnation, these brutal incursions continue as I write.

Can you imagine the horror these Africans have to live with, seeing their villages burned, their men killed and their women raped whenever a group of bandits choose to pay them a visit?

To make things more interesting, the Arab rulers of Sudan are bankrolled and kept in power by Saudi Arabia, who obviously control oil supplies to the West and also use their oil money to promote the Wahhabi sect of Islam, which is responsible for terrorism. Because of the political clout of the Saudis, the West has been unable to do anything about the atrocities in Darfur.

The moral of this story, if that is that right word, is that a totalitarian government can benefit from driving out a minority population and giving their land to its supporters.

### Takeover by Liberation – Tibet and Georgia

Sometimes a country has great mineral wealth and a neighbour can see the benefit of adding another province to their country so as to control the production. The way they go about this is either to march in on a pretext of already having title to the country or, if they already have some of their people living there, they stir up discontent among their own settlers, saying they are discriminated against or whatever.

The advantage an aggressor has in this situation is that they can act quickly and take over before the rest of the world has even met to discuss the situation. Then possession is nine-tenths of the law. Once they are in, they ship in loads of settlers until they can win any national vote. This tactic is almost impossible to reverse. China used it 60 years ago to take over Tibet for its minerals and is still there.

Russia used the same trick recently to invade Georgia on the pretext of protecting its ethnic citizens in South Ossetia. The real story is far more complex, with Georgia being ruled by a government brought in by the US and bribed to join NATO. If Georgia were to become a member of NATO, for the Russians it would be like the US having Russian missiles in Cuba – totally unacceptable.

But the plot goes further than this because, as Russia is beginning to feel the financial benefit of a relatively free economy and flex its muscles, it is finding that its huge reserves of gas and oil give it more power than its tanks. The way it uses this power is that it has set up a decentralised network of oil and gas pipelines across Russia which deliver to Eastern Europe and the West. If a country gets on the wrong side of Russia, this vital fuel supply is cut off, as it was recently when

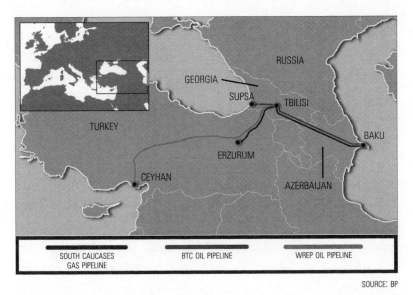

SOURCE: BP

the state-owned gas firm Gazprom turned off the taps to Ukraine.

To get out of this potential stranglehold, the West, through the oil company BP, has built a series of pipelines from Azerbaijan and the landlocked Caspian Sea ports in the East, across Georgia to the Georgian Black Sea port of Supsa and south into Turkey, where they lead to the Mediterranean port of Ceyhan. This group of pipelines carries over 1.2 million barrels of oil a day and is the second biggest in the world.

Oddly, when the Russians invaded Georgia, they shut the port of Supsa and if they had come south just a few more miles they would have controlled the oil flow to Turkey. So the West, once again, would have been dependent on Russian goodwill for its oil.

As a general rule, the way to tell who is doing what in international affairs is to look at who benefits, given that the media don't always give the full story.

### MAINTAINING POWER BY FORCE – ZIMBABWE

When British politicians handed over Rhodesia to a sham government in 1980, the die was cast for civil war and mass murder. There are two tribes in the country, which was quickly renamed Zimbabwe: the Mashona and the Matabele. There are more of the Mashona, so when there were elections all the tribespeople voted for their chief and the biggest tribe won. The chief who became legitimised by this election was the terrorist Robert Mugabe and he then set about making his position secure by killing huge numbers of Matabele.

Zimbabwe quickly collapsed from being the breadbasket of Africa to needing international aid as Mugabe handed out jobs and land to his cronies, who promptly set about collecting the most bribes they could squeeze from their new employment and stripping the assets from their farms. Within a few years the people were starving and looking for a scapegoat. To save his own position Mugabe blamed first the Matabele then the British government. But he still had a problem: the people were desperate for something better and he needed to cling to his job or face trial for any number of offences against the nation.

What could he do but strengthen the army and police to stifle discontent? And when elections finally started to

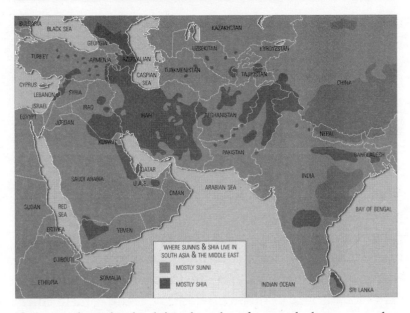

WHERE SUNNIS & SHIA LIVE IN
SOUTH ASIA & THE MIDDLE EAST

MOSTLY SUNNI

MOSTLY SHIA

threaten him he had his bands of armed thugs murder and intimidate the opposition. That is how tyrants stay in power. He is still there at the head of a starving country backed only by guns.

DIVIDE AND RULE – THE MIDDLE EAST

Like much of the world, until well into the last century the Middle East was divided up more into tribal lands than countries with borders. The British Empire, which controlled a great part of the world before the First World War, developed a technique for ruling foreign lands which had assets that were of value to the British economy. What they did was establish a country by drawing borders in such a way that the inhabitants of the new country were divided on ethnic lines. One group was always smaller than the others. Then the British would put the smaller group in charge as their officials. This had the obvious effect of ensuring loyalty among the minority as if there were a mass rebellion not only would the minority be treated as collaborators but they would also lose all power and benefit to the leaders of the larger group.

This trick was used in Iraq, where the result was the struggles between Shia and Sunni Muslims, in Northern Ireland with the Protestants and Catholic Christians, and in many other places.

The one thing I want you to take away with you from this chapter is that when it comes to dealing with civilians in a country you are visiting you must trust no one. The vast majority of people the world over are OK. Treat them decently and they will behave the same towards you. Because that is how people the world over are brought up; in the main they get along. The problem comes when you are in their country for a reason they do not approve of. In that case they will often pretend to be friendly for reasons I outlined above but, and this is important, you can never know what they have in mind. It only takes one to be looking for glory, revenge or reward and you can kiss goodbye to your next leave.

Treat them all as well as you can, but remember, they are all potential enemies.

# Chapter Ten

# Weapons And Killing Techniques

Here we'll look at how to make effective use of any weapon you may come across: knives, pistols, grenades or whatever comes to hand. There are two basic principles to bear in mind: minimum risk and use what you have.

## MINIMUM RISK

Although it is valid in all forms of conflict, to the best of my knowledge, the idea is never taught that the whole point of combat is to kill the opposition at minimum risk to yourself. There is no honour involved, sadly, nor moral argument. Let me illustrate this in a way which is slightly ridiculous but you might remember, because it is very important.

If the enemy is approaching you from a distance, then the first thing you want to do is call in an air strike while he is a hundred miles away. If he gets closer then call in artillery or mortars. Still coming and you are now at personal risk. You might try a heavy machine gun at

2,000 metres (6,550 feet) and then rifles at 400 metres (1,300 feet). If you still cannot stop him, at 50 metres (160 feet) use a pistol and then a grenade. Closer than that and you are going to get personal and the risk increases again. Close up and personal, use a spear or bayonet, then a club, then a knife, and as a last resort fight with your bare hands.

Do you see where I am going here? There is no need to take more risk of damage than the situation and your equipment requires. Kill safely and at a distance when you can. Only kill close when you have to on the grounds of safety or silence. This does not contradict the principle of opening fire at point-blank range in ambushes as this is the maximum effective distance in that situation.

## USE WHAT YOU HAVE

When you are on the run, the chances are you will be down to no more than a rifle/pistol and grenades even if you are switched on. A knife or less if you are not. Have you heard the expression 'Proper Planning Prevents Piss-Poor Performance'? It is referred to in the British Army as the Six Ps and you need to remember it. The most important decisions relating to survival in the field are made, not as you climb out of a burning chopper or break heroically out of nick, but the last time you are in base camp before the cock-up.

In this section I'm going to teach you how to kill safely and efficiently with a range of weapons both standard-issue and improvised. Some of this is a little messy, but needs must when the Devil drives. Before we come to that, I want to get across to you a couple more ideas which might affect how you live your life. The first of these is that weapons do not kill people, people do. This phrase is often used in support of the legal right to own a weapon as a civilian, but I don't give a damn about that. What it means for you is that it doesn't matter that your opponent has the latest Beretta assault rifle and you have a rock. If you know what you are doing and can get close, he is dead. On a more likely note, a man carrying a high-tech rifle dies just as well when shot with an old bolt-action rifle or home-made shotgun as he does when hit with something smarter. So don't be fazed by any lack in your arsenal. You are the real weapon. A gun is just a tool.

The other idea I want to share with you is that frightened dogs bite. This is why small and timid boys in Civvy Street carry guns and knives. They are afraid to be without them. However tough they look, they are afraid inside. This type are often on the end of a lead attached to a ferocious-looking dog. The dog is not an expression of how tough they are inside, it is there to protect them. I am simply telling you this to make it clear that, by contrast, a balanced soldier, indeed a balanced person, will not kill for the sake of it, not kill out of anger and certainly not for pleasure, but only when the occasion requires it. On the other hand, when the time comes to kill, it should be like switching off an electric light.

My final point is that the first time you kill someone it may seem a big deal according to the ethics of the society in which you have been raised and other circumstances. You may have already seen some action in the sense of making contact with the enemy and you will know that there is a world of difference between soldiers who have been in a shooting match and those who have not. It does make a change in their heads and they are much steadier afterwards. And here I am only talking of a contact where you and the enemy are shooting at each other from a distance and, as is the common way of things, where you cannot actually see who is shooting at you.

In a similar but stronger way, the first kill you make, where you know for a fact you shot or stabbed a real person yourself, changes you too. As a rule, a man goes quiet for a day or two as he comes to terms with it, then he is OK again and the second kill is no more than squashing a mosquito. I have no idea how a woman reacts as I have never seen a woman kill anyone. Not literally anyway.

What we will do now is go through the list of weapons you may have access to while on the run and show you the best way to kill the opposition with them without being either caught or killed. You may already be experienced in the use of some of these weapons but I believe you could still learn something useful.

## BODY ARMOUR

There are two types of body armour: the big, bulky sort, usually called a flak jacket, and the thin, hidden sort, sometimes called a bulletproof vest. If you can see that your target is wearing a flak jacket, a pistol or a knife is no good against it and you must go for the head or groin to be effective.

When on the run, you probably won't be wearing a flak jacket because they are heavy and do not generally stop rifle bullets. Nevertheless, I will say a few words here you might want to remember as they apply to both you *and* anyone you are wanting to kill who is wearing body armour.

Flak jackets are very good for stopping shrapnel splinters when grenades, mortars or other bombs are coming down, and they are fine if the people shooting at them have pistols, but unless they have heavy steel plates in the front they do not stop rifle bullets. By wearing such an obvious suit of armour, anyone you might want to kill is warning you what will work and what will not. That is quite good of them, if you think about it.

When you are working undercover, if you wear visible armour you will look pretty obvious – besides warning the opposition what will work on you – so the choice is between no armour and hidden armour. A hidden bulletproof vest will stop a knife or a pistol bullet aimed at your chest and probably save your life. Wear one if you can. A bulletproof vest stops penetration but not the painful punch of a pistol bullet.

## FIGHTING KNIFE

We are not talking here about the sailors in Marseilles for whom knife fighting used to be an art form. The whole idea of every single action I am going to show you with each of these weapons, and indeed with your fists later, is not to give the other guy a chance. If you give the guy a chance, like squaring up for a boxing match, over time you will win about one fight in two. In the field you need to win every single encounter or you die.

If you do end up facing someone with a knife in his hand, shoot him. Joking apart, we had better cover this just in case. There are several schools of knife fighting and, as a long-time sword fencer, I prefer to lead with the knife hand rather than hold it close to protect it and fend off the other guy with a coat around my leading arm. This last detail is from the Spanish style: they used to fight with a cloak and a sort of penknife with a two-foot blade!

In a knife fight, the balance of weight between the front and rear legs is not as important as in boxing because you do not need to generate power in the strike, just speed. But you should still lead with one foot and move by sliding the rear foot first to move backwards and the front foot first to go forwards. This keeps your feet far enough apart to maintain your balance.

Always hold your knife with the blade projecting out from the top of your fist as opposed to downwards like a dagger. The thumb should run on top of the handle and point towards the tip of the blade. Your four fingers should be wrapped around the handle. This grip combines firmness with flexibility.

The most important factor in any face-to-face fighting is distance. In boxing, karate, fencing and other disciplines, you absolutely must keep your opponent far enough away so that he cannot hit you without taking a step. Where an opponent is within this distance, he can move to hit you before you have time to react, however quick you are. This step takes him time and gives you time to react and block or counterstrike.

In the fastest of all combat forms, fencing, the attacker develops terrific speed over one step of the leading foot to close the 'fencing distance' and this movement is called a lunge. The way you keep your distance in a knife fight, or any other type of fight, is by what is called retiring on stance. To come close, your opponent must step forward and this is your chance to strike while he is moving and usually off balance. Wait for him to move towards you and begin to stretch to stab or cut, then, stepping back to maintain the safe distance, bring up your knife inside his guard and cut deeply into his wrist with a sort of hooking action. This will stop him as, with the tendons gone, he cannot hold a knife.

All weapons work best when the other person does not know you have one. Think about it: if you see someone swaggering about with a big knife on their belt, you know either that you should leave them alone or what you are up against. Anyone without a knife will probably leave them alone or creep up with a rock rather than just start an argument. Anyone with a pistol will keep them at a distance until they choose to shoot them. Most of the advantage to the knife owner is therefore lost.

You should keep your knife out of sight until you are ready to use it. Do not threaten with a knife and then put it down or away as you lose the surprise value. There are fancy shoulder holsters for knives but a normal sheath on the belt but turned to your spine so it is covered by your coat is as good as anything. It is possible to turn the normal sheath of a knife upside down on your belt so the blade points upwards and the handle down. This can make the knife fit into your waist and be less noticeable.

If someone jumps you and wrestles you to the ground, they don't have a knife. Try to headbutt them to gain the initiative, then reach to draw your knife and in the one movement strike straight to the centre of the chest and jerk or twist the knife inside the body to make a big cut and kill quickly. If your opponent is wearing body armour, aim for the groin. It is almost always unprotected and a knife aimed straight up from under the crotch will put anyone out of action immediately, although it will not kill them for half an hour unless you catch the main femoral artery on the inside of the thigh.

When approaching someone from behind with the aim of taking them down you are better using a rock or piece of wood to knock them out than try the more risky action of killing them with a knife. Only use a knife in an attack of this kind if your opponent is wearing a helmet.

Given he has a helmet and no body armour, keep your head leaned back, safely away from flailing arms, then reach quickly around the head with one arm. As you grip and pull back, he will always raise his arms to grab yours. As he does so, reach under his elbows to his front and slide the knife into the lower chest aiming up. A long knife will reach the heart and kill instantly while a shorter knife will have to be twisted around a little to rip the lungs and kill by loss of blood there.

If he has a helmet and body armour and is standing, then come up behind, grab the collar in one hand and stamp on the back of the knee with the opposite foot. As he falls back, guide him with the collar hand to fall to your side. Step around him and push the knife into his throat or groin.

If he has a helmet and body armour but is sitting, turn the knife so the blade points down from your fist gripping it around the handle. Strike hard and straight down into the side of his neck inside the collar. A long knife will kill instantly as it penetrates the heart from above but it must be accurate rather than stick in the collar of his body armour.

In a situation where you end up struggling with someone and they are wearing body armour and you do not want to lower your guard arm to strike for the groin, you need to trip him and go for the neck. A long knife should go straight down into his chest as above but with a short knife stab into the neck from the side and with the blade facing forward. Cut forward and you will sever the carotid artery and he will die almost instantly. This is a useful technique to master and remember for killing men and food animals.

Your first kill with a knife may surprise you at how much people bleed. Try not to get yourself or your knife covered in blood as it makes your grip slippery.

## PISTOL

I have said elsewhere that pistols are useless in combat. Well, compared with a rifle they are. They have no range, no hitting power and no useful rate of fire. But when used properly they are a damn sight better than nothing. In the situations we are looking at here, your pistol may be the best and only friend you have, so we had better show you how to use one properly.

You need to know what a particular weapon is capable of, then use it within that capability to achieve your aim. A rifle will shoot a mile or two but you can't hit anything at that distance. On a shooting range you will be able to hit a man-sized target in the chest at 300 metres (980 feet) but when you are in a combat situation you will be lucky to see a bit of the target, maybe the head or the head and shoulders for a moment or two while you and he are both moving. And, more interestingly, he, or one of his mates, may well be shooting at you. This ruins the concentration and all the instructions about breathing and so on go out the window – the first few times anyway.

So when you are in a combat situation I always say to consider rifle fire at more than 50 metres (160 feet) to be suppressing fire which just keeps their heads down or spoils their aim. Even though there is plenty of stopping power at much greater range, you just will not get enough hits. Used wrongly, this type of fire prevents you getting to grips with the enemy and lets them get away to tell stories of how good they were. If you want to kill the enemy with a rifle, then let them get within 50 metres before telling them you are there by shooting them. Better is 30 metres (100 feet). This, clearly, is not for those of a nervous disposition.

With a pistol you will probably be trained to shoot at 50 metres on the range. Consider this to be the extreme range at which you will engage the target in an emergency such as they are pointing a rifle at you.

A pistol, remember, has a barrel of about 10–15cm (4–6 inches), whereas a rifle has a 40–50cm (16–20in) barrel, so movement of a pistol's barrel tip is magnified about five times. There is also no way to hold a pistol into your shoulder to prevent swing or shake, so of course it is less accurate than a rifle.

And a pistol only has a tiny barrel length to accelerate the bullet up to speed without breaking your wrist, so there is a severe limit to the power that can be built into the round. The magnum round is mythic but actually it is too powerful to use in a pistol because of the recoil and yet still pitifully weak compared with a rifle. A pistol chambered for a magnum round is so big and heavy you might as well have a rifle.

A rifle bullet will go through both sides of a flak jacket and mince the body inside. A pistol bullet will not go through one side. Enough said about penetration, I think.

Now I have destroyed your confidence in pistols, let's

look at what they can do well. A pistol can be hidden. That is probably its best feature. You can draw it quickly when you know how. You can also take down multiple targets at wide angles, say in a room or street, much faster than you can swing a heavy rifle around. So, for very close work, when no body armour is involved, a pistol does have the edge on a rifle.

What is the best pistol to use? Well, like rifles, I think the goon holding it is more important than the weapon by a long way. There are two main types of pistol: the revolver and the semi-automatic.

A revolver holds only five or six rounds in the revolving magazine chambers and these take a while to reload even with the fancy ejection systems and multiple loading some have. On the plus side, I have never known a revolver jam. Which is very comforting.

## REVOLVER

Revolvers come in two flavours: the single-action and the double-action. The single-action needs you to pull the hammer back before firing by pulling the trigger. This is how the old cowboy six-shooters worked. The double-action uses the action of pulling the trigger back to cock the hammer then the final part of the trigger movement releases it to fire. Double action allows repeated firing with one hand but the pressure required on the trigger to cock the hammer tends to pull the weapon off aim so it is far better to hand-cock the first shot. Then you can hold the trigger back and fan the hammer for repeat shots like a gunslinger if you want to look the part.

## SEMI-AUTOMATIC

Often referred to wrongly but usefully as automatics, semi-automatic pistols fire one shot every time the trigger is depressed. The top slide comes back and kicks out the old case, then forward on a spring to load the next round from a spring-driven magazine in the handgrip. Most automatics are made so the slide stays back when the magazine is empty so you know this useful fact.

The semi-automatic is slightly less reliable than a revolver but pretty good so long as you keep it clean and tap the rounds to the back of the magazine. The advantage of an automatic is that you can change a magazine of seven to thirteen rounds in a moment, so you are not vulnerable for long. Of course, my opinion is that you should not really be in a situation where you need a second mag if you are doing it right. Remember, this is all about surprise and keeping the odds on your side, not a shooting competition. My favourite automatic is a Beretta 92FS, which is a pretty thing with a double-stacked 15-round mag of 9mm rounds. A close second is the .45 Colt, which, I must admit, does stop a man so long as he is not wearing body armour.

Both revolvers and automatics come in a multitude of designs along the two common themes and chambered to fire rounds of .22 inch to .45 inch. In Europe, 9mm is very popular for the automatic as it allows more rounds in the mag, while .45 is the US favourite because, although it only has seven rounds, it does stop a man, or a horse, with one shot.

Aside from the .45, look at all pistols as requiring a head shot. Remember the rhyme, 'Two in the head and you know that he's dead.' Some say three. So from that point of view there is little to choose between them.

You have probably seen magic silencers on TV just like atomic hand grenades. Actual silencers, while very useful, are not as quiet as you might think. A silencer does not work on a rifle because the bullet travels faster than sound and makes a sonic crack which is nearly as loud as the detonation of the round. A pistol, on the other hand, because it is firing a (usually) heavy round slowly, does not make a crack. So there is a start to work on.

If you fit a silencer on a revolver, there is a gap between the magazine cylinder and the barrel through which gas escapes with a crack and a flash in the dark. There is no efficient way around this that I can see.

On an automatic, the silencer stops the flash from the barrel but when the slide comes back gas and sound come out of the ejection opening as the empty cartridge is ejected. The only way to stop this is to make the pistol single-shot, and with this modification the weapon can be fairly quiet.

You can carry a pistol or a grenade in your pocket but if I saw a bulge like that I would be wary. To get through a search, carry a small pistol like the Walther PP .22-inch automatic and slip it down the front of your pants. Most men will not search another man's crotch in public. Failing this, wear your holster so the weapon is against your spine, where it is more likely to be missed when a searcher 'pats down' the sides of your body.

There are two useful types of concealed holster – the side and the shoulder – and each has advantages and disadvantages. The side holster on your hip sticks out more than is easy to hide and a coat over the top can foul a quick draw. An alternative is to wear the holster to the rear and reach round further. A quick draw with a side holster is accurate because the pistol is moving forward and up as it reaches the aiming point. This means you will be good for line but poor for elevation and probably hit the target somewhere between foot and head.

A shoulder holster is much better for hiding the weapon but here a quick draw means a cross-draw, where the pistol is moving across your body as it comes to the aim, and this is not accurate at all. The best thing to do if you have to draw in a hurry is draw and point the pistol at the ceiling, then bring your aim down on to the target. So you pay your money and take your choice. I like shoulder holsters as I don't like people to know I am carrying and I always try to avoid a quick-draw contest.

To sum up, keep your pistol clean so you can rely on it when needed. Draw your pistol only when you are ready to use it or you need to put the fear of God into someone. Shoot only when you cannot miss, and go for the head. When he goes down, walk up and make sure with a knife. One shot in a public place will be ignored. Two shots start a panic.

## GRENADE

I make no excuses for favouring the shrapnel hand grenade above all other weapons for infantry or clandestine combat. To be clear, by hand grenade, I mean an explosive device of some kind which is thrown at the opposition. This is distinct from a rifle grenade, which is fired from a rifle with a blank round propellant. Some people are surprised to learn that the purpose of a grenade, whether hand or rifle, is not actually to kill people. It is to stun them long enough to get in close and kill them with a knife, rifle or bayonet. This it does very effectively.

There are a great many types of hand grenade but for our purposes they fall into three types: shrapnel grenades, which explode and drive pieces of shrapnel in all directions, phosphorus grenades, which are supposedly for making smoke to signal but really are for burning people's lungs out, and concussion grenades, which are a modern concept of the non-lethal weapon.

Shrapnel grenades used to be a chunk of iron, something like a pineapple in shape, with an ounce of explosive inside and a short fuse. The best known was the Mills 36 grenade, which was such an excellent piece of kit it remained in service from 1915 to 1972 with little change. Around 70 million were made for use in the First World War alone.

The designer, William Mills, was a golf-club maker from Sunderland, UK, and he made the 36 to replace an earlier form of stick grenade which was proving difficult to throw from the trenches. Originally, the 36 had a seven-second fuse so it could also be used as a rifle grenade with a range of around 150 metres (500 feet) but when thrown by hand this often resulted in some brave Kraut tossing it back, so the fuse was reduced to four seconds for hand-thrown grenades. A competent thrower can toss a 36 around 30 metres (100 feet) but the shrapnel travels further than this, so you do need to take cover.

Eventually, it was concluded that the fact a 36 exploded into a few big chunks was a disadvantage and the British Army opted for the L2 series instead. These are lemon-shaped and the cast-iron body is replaced by coiled brittle wire in a tin shell, which results in everyone in the area getting a number of small pieces.

There is a Russian hand grenade which is very similar to the 36 and also has a four-second fuse. In Mozambique, I once had one of these go off a metre from my shoulder and 13 pieces of it hit me all down my right side and, for some reason, the sole of my left foot. The pieces were all less than a quarter of an inch long and the impact felt like a hard blow with the knee or fist. It did not put me out of action and I was able to take down the thrower and a number of his friends. I didn't say I wasn't pissed off. One piece ran along my right brow over the eye, a piece cut into the back of my right arm and took in some filthy clothing material which became infected, a number of pieces went into my right thigh and some into the sole of my left foot, which I had unthinkingly crossed behind me, being belly down and trying to dig in with my teeth. The sole of the foot was by far the most uncomfortable, particularly when the pieces were cut out. I was conscious of the needles and scalpel scraping on the bones in my foot. You can't look soft when there are pretty nurses about, though.

Why didn't the grenade kill me? Well, I said above that is not what they are for and, although they will often kill someone if they go off close enough, you should not rely on this but always follow up with a decisive attack.

All hand grenades have a fuse inside and a striker to set them off. The striker is held back against a spring by some kind of lever and this lever is held in place by a pin. As I explained earlier, taking the pin out does nothing if you hold the lever in place, and if you do not use the grenade you can replace the pin later. Once you release the lever, however, a striker pin is driven down on to a detonator by a spring and you have four seconds to get the grenade somewhere where it will not hurt you.

Grenades, like artillery shells, work a lot better if they explode in the air above the target. If they land on soft ground this soaks up some of the blast; hard ground focuses the blast upwards so that only people close by get the benefit, but with an air explosion everyone gets their fair share. This, by the way, is why we do not dig our foxholes under trees. There are few things more depressing than, when you have dug a fine trench or foxhole to shelter in, having a tree branch above you detonate an incoming mortar shell.

Four seconds is a lot longer than it sounds, so if you are close you might want to release the lever and count to one or two before tossing the grenade. With practice you will get a feel for the timing and be able to get the grenade to explode in the air among the opposition.

Phosphorus grenades are unlawful and banned by the Geneva Convention for use against troops. This is why they are referred to as 'white smoke' in the manuals and quartermaster's stores. They explode with a soft pop and throw up a cloud of white smoke which could, indeed, be seen from a circling aircraft. Alternatively, the smoke could be used to burn the lungs out of the opposition. Among the smoke are lots of little chunks of phosphorus which are burning and continue to burn whatever you do to them. They will burn right through your flesh, so do be careful with them.

The main benefit of phosphorus grenades is in clearing bunkers, where if you toss a shrapnel grenade in it might fall in a hole or somehow be shielded from the occupants.

This does not happen with phosphorus and the people in the bunker either die inside or come out blind, burning and choking.

As white smoke, phosphorus is a very useful signalling tool, which is why tanks also carry phosphorus rounds for signalling to aircraft and other troop formations when their five radios all pack in. Right.

You may have heard of the 'thunderflash', a very loud firecracker used to simulate grenades in training exercises. These are great fun at parties but of limited use in combat. On the other hand, a stun grenade, correctly named the G60, and often called a flash-bang, is the mother of all thunderflashes. It has a sonic shock of 160 decibels and a flash of 300,000 candlepower, so if you toss one into a room which has both good guys and bad guys in it they will be stunned long enough for you to walk in and shoot the bad guys.

The G60 first came to public attention in 1980 when the British SAS stormed the Iranian Embassy to release hostages taken by the terrorists inside. They were able to kill the terrorists and rescue the hostages in part by the use of stun grenades.

Now remember I am not teaching you to use grenades in combat here. What I want to do is give you an idea of how to use them in a situation where you are undercover or on the run. Grenades can come in really handy in time of need.

If a crowd gathers around you with hostile intent, don't start shooting as you may lose your pistol. Toss a grenade over the heads of the men closest and duck. This will make them stop and think. Repeat if required.

If someone is following you, particularly at night, dog-leg back and ambush the path you have come along. Toss them a grenade from cover and time it to go off in the air. This will take them down and not give away your position to any other watchers.

If you need to spring an ambush at night and alone, lay your weapon down by your side and hold a grenade. Take out the pin and toss it at the right moment then you will have time to pick up your weapon and be ready to shoot as the grenade explodes.

### GARROTTE

A garrotte is a very simple tool for strangling someone to death. It consists of just a length of something flexible and strong, like fishing line, wire or a scarf, with a handle at each end. It is popped over the head from behind and pulled tight. The word comes, via French, from Spain, where at one time it was used in executions, very often before burning if the executioner was sympathetic or well paid.

Although quiet and fairly clean, a garrotte is not normally a weapon of choice because there are few occasions when a knife, rock or other club is not better. The problem is getting the cord round someone's neck without it catching on their helmet or them getting their hands in the way.

Attacking someone, say a sentry, from behind, you are better hitting them over the head with a rock or club if they do not have a helmet on. And if they do, a knife is more certainly effective. The big problem with a garrotte is that the target may just get their hand up in time to catch the cord, in which case it is useless and the target can cry out. There may just be a time when you need to kill quietly and leave no blood so you can hide the deed or perhaps you do not have a knife.

You can make this weapon with a piece of strong, stiff cord or wire. It really needs to be stiff so that when put over the target's head from behind it can be guided into position. You need to fit a handle to each end so you have something to pull hard on.

The way to use the garrotte is to creep up behind the target, lower the wire quickly yet carefully over the head, then pull sharply back. Drop the target with pressure to the back of the knee if they are standing, then place your knee behind the neck so you can get a good pull. They will pass out in a few minutes and die in about six or eight.

## SPEAR

A spear is a weapon of last resort when you have nothing else and have to be prepared to fight face to face. If you have the chance, as I said earlier, always try to get the jump on the opposition, but there just could be a time when you are in danger of bumping into someone coming the other way at night on a track or whatever.

You can make a very serviceable spear with a length of bamboo or wood 1.5–2 metres (5–6? feet) long. This may sound primitive but if you sharpen the end and then blacken it in a fire to make it harder you will have a weapon more than capable of sliding into someone's belly. For head-on combat it is far superior to a knife or machete.

The way to use a spear in this sort of situation is to hold it near the back end with your preferred hand and this hand stuck out behind you with the spear lying level and pointing to your front, supported by your other hand just in front of your body. The reason for this odd stance is that when you come to use it you can extend the spear forward very quickly and with a lot of force by pushing your rear hand forward. Old soldiers may know that this is cribbed from the art of bayonet fencing. A similar trick was performed by holding the sling of the rifle where it was attached to the stock and forcing the weapon out in front of you at great speed. This gave you a much greater reach than your opponent.

## CLUB

Any sort of stick which is heavy at least at one end will do nicely as a club if it is used properly. A blow to the head will kill or render the target unconscious but so will a firm blow between the shoulder blades as this affects the nerves in the spine. This can be useful if the target is wearing a helmet. Even if he is not rendered unconscious, he will be on the floor and unable to argue effectively.

Many people do not think to use a club to break limbs or paralyse them. A firm blow to the lower arm will break it, particularly from above so that it hits the two bones together. If your opponent is wearing body armour or has a shield, a useful ploy is to bend and swipe sideways at the legs or knee. Knees are delicate at the best of times, so a smack across the side of the knee with a stout stick will disable or even break the leg.

In a civilian interaction, it is important not to target the head unless you intend to kill, as knocking someone unconscious is not like TV and is in reality a hair's breadth from killing them.

Many years ago, I was driving along a country lane in Derbyshire when a car came up behind me and started tailgating. Now I am quite boring and drive pretty steadily, so I slowed to let the chap get past. This must have upset him as he came past me and slid his car to a halt, blocking the road only a couple of yards to my front. Then he got out with his eyes like saucers and screaming, so I got out too as I didn't want to be caught sitting in a car and at a disadvantage by what looked like a crazy man.

He stepped up and took a swing at me. You will recall I said about distance a way back? So I just rocked back a little and his punch, a swinging haymaker, came across in front of me. He tried again, so I stepped back again with the same result. The third time he swung at me I stepped back and let his fist go past before rocking forward to smack him across the cheek with a steel bar I had concealed in my hand.

He went down screaming like a stuck pig, so I got back in the car and drove off.

There were a number of interesting results from this interaction. The first was that I was charged with assault. When people, who later become witnesses, see an unusual event they see what they expect to see. At least that is what they remember when they try to make sense of it later. A number of cars had come to a halt behind us and the witnesses there thought they saw me punching the guy as he was the one who was injured.

When it came to court the whole thing was sorted out, I was found not guilty and my little crowbar, a useful tool for tightening the load on my truck, was returned to me.

## BOOBY-TRAPS

When you are on the run, the main purpose of a booby-trap is to slow the pursuit. Make them more careful. You can make a very serviceable booby-trap by tying a grenade to a tree at shin height. Loosen the pin, then tie a cord to the pin and across the path to another anchor point. The next person along the path will get such a fright.

If the conditions are right, you can use a grenade to set off a whole load of fuel or whatever is handy. This can be quite distracting in town or country.

Without explosives, and always in a hurry, you are pretty much limited to wooden spikes. Dig a small pit and put stakes in the bottom, then cover it so the next person drops with their whole weight on to the spikes. In close cover and at night you might be able to rig a stake like a spear for the next person to walk on to.

Another useful tool is the bullet mine. If you have time to prepare and expect to need to stop someone following you, either draw a few small anti-personnel mines from stores or make them yourself. The easiest way is to get a length of metal tube a few inches long and of the right diameter to just accept a pistol or rifle round. Get another tube which fits over this and block the end with a plate and a spike. A shotgun cartridge works very well indeed.

When pressure, say from someone standing on it, is applied to the end of the narrow tube, it forces the percussion cap at the back of the cartridge on to the spike like a firing pin and fires the round. Ouch!

Bury this toy pointing up in a path and it will make everyone after the next passer-by walk very carefully indeed. The nice thing about it is that it weighs almost nothing.

## Chapter Eleven

# Unarmed Combat

If all else fails and you have nothing to shoot, stab or hit the opposition with, you are going to have to use your bare hands.

I can't make a seasoned, experienced streetfighter of you through a book because it takes one-to-one instruction and lots of practice. But I can put you so far ahead of the opposition that you will be able to beat anyone you are likely to meet quite easily. Provided you are not in a situation where the law is an issue and you have to go soft on them. It is much easier to kill or disable someone than it is to arrest them or use minimum force to stop them robbing your grandmother.

Remember, we are not talking about a boxing ring, gymnasium or dojo here. We are talking about coming up against someone in the boys' room of a bar, a prison cell or the back street of some God-forsaken mud town.

All you have to do is stop them. There are no rules.

Almost every time you fight you will be up against an amateur who has not fought to kill before. This gives you a massive advantage. The main reason for this is that there are very few men who are trained to fight with their hands and men who can fight very rarely do. Let me try to give you some background so this sticks in your head.

Unlike on TV, where everyone is a martial arts expert, in the real world when two guys fight in a bar or anywhere else it is generally a pitiful sight. As a prison guard, conscript soldier or terrorist, they may well never even have fought another guy in the school yard. Amateurs in bars swing at each other or try to stick a glass in someone's face in a way that any kind of boxer, martial artist or trained fighter would laugh at. It really is the difference between a fighter and a comedian. On top of this, in bars the fighters are almost always drunk too. How convenient is that!

The two main practical differences between trained fighters, such as competent boxers and marital artists above a certain level, and the other sort are that fighters are very hard to hit because of their dodging or blocking and they also hit a damned sight harder. They are also harder to knock down if you can hit them because they are permanently in a balanced stance. Someone not trained to punch, for example, almost always swings at you and connects with a slap like a girl – unless you are very unlucky and they catch you just right. If they fail to connect, they often fall over or at least stagger.

When I was a youngster, I used to moonlight in bars and clubs as a bouncer or doorman. In those days you didn't need a licence, just to be able to smack the troublemakers and kick them outside. In years of doing this sort of work in the UK, Europe and South Africa, I never came across one man who could fight. This is why I could throw out rugby teams and ex-special forces guys in Durban nightclubs and take down sailors with knives in some rough houses. I even took a pistol off a guy in a fight over a rather lovely girl in one nightclub.

And it isn't just that they were mostly civilians either. All the old soldiers will know the dreaded 'Sennelager Strip'. Situated near Paderborn in north Germany, this long row of bars and whorehouses catering mainly to squaddies was a must-visit centre for tank soldiers posted there and soldiers from regiments of all kinds and nations on exercises.

One night I was drinking in a bar there and a young tanky I knew, a nice kid, was entertaining his girlfriend when a bunch of seven 'hard men' came in and started picking on him. He and his girl were playing pool and the weekend warriors started knocking the balls about and calling his girl names. He moved her away and still they were harassing the couple quite nastily.

I went over, smacked one of the guys and we kicked off. In a couple of minutes I put six of them out of action when a huge Kraut I had ignored picked me up from behind and threw me through the window. Fortunately, the shutters were down so I went through the glass and bounced off the shutters back into the room with only a scratched elbow.

The last one was still standing and would not go down, however hard I hit him. I was afraid of killing him – this would be a shame for him as he was a plucky guy and a shame for me for obvious reasons. Eventually, he went down and I checked him over for serious damage. He was just pissed and very tough.

I helped him up and, as is often the way with soldiers, there were no hard feelings. He offered me a drink and showed me a hole in his cheek he could put a couple of fingers through. I had needed to beat his face to a pulp to make him lie down.

I'm not telling you about this little bout because I want you to think I am a tough guy. I know I can fight and I don't need to impress anyone. What I want you to realise is that here were a bunch of guys who were very fit, not at all shy, and among the toughest soldiers in the world. *But they were not trained to fight without weapons.* So, in a fight against a trained fighter, they had no chance whatsoever. No more than someone who cannot drive can beat a racing driver on the track. The same applies with knives, pistols, rifles and pretty much anything you can swing at someone.

To balance things out a bit, let me tell you another story which reinforces my point, although it shows me in a less heroic light. I had been out drinking all night while on leave in a city in the north of England. I came out of a nightclub well pissed with a rather gentle civilian friend. I don't remember where we were going but we went into some back streets and crossed a car park. There were a bunch of young men there spoiling for trouble and we were it.

My friend rolled over on the floor without putting up much of a struggle but I did my best despite the beer and took a really good pasting. It turned out to be the Royal Marines boxing team. Which sort of shows why you don't drink and fight or, if you have to fight, don't try it on with boxers. If you want to learn to fight, take boxing lessons as there is nothing better.

To take down a group of men, you have to be able to disable each man with one, or at most two, touches. Then you can move on to the next quickly without giving them time to climb all over you. This is impossible with boxers as their guard is so good. And those guys could box, which is why I could make no headway at all. As an aside, it is really strange for boxers to pick fights. Who knows what was happening?

It's time to look in detail at fighting with your bare hands. Imagine any situation where you may have to fight without weapons: a bar, a rest-room, a street or whatever. What they all have in common is that some guy wants to hurt you and he is pretty close. There is little time for either of you to think. He may not be capable of thinking, but I hope you are or you will lose.

There may be other civilians around and they are almost certainly going to be frozen in a state of shock as the confrontation develops. Remember, most people never see this sort of thing in real life.

The most important thing to remember is that the man attacking you is almost certainly not sure what to do. He will almost certainly swing a clumsy punch or kick at you from wherever his feet happen to be at the time. This will leave him way off balance and open to anything you might want to do with him.

What I shall do, therefore, is first tell you a little about attacking someone, then I shall go into how to defend against an attack. We are not by any means talking 'self-defence' here, we are talking about crippling people, but I am going to show you that you are better turning any confrontation into a defending situation because it is much easier to deal with.

A person attacking you has committed to a move and is probably pretty slow so you can see what he is doing and deal with it. The theory of attacking someone is pretty easy to learn but you do have to avoid giving your opponent the defending advantage. This does require a bit of thought and a lot of practice with your mates.

## FIGHTING STANCE

Learn to keep your weight evenly spread between your feet so you can move quickly and are less easy to trip. A boxer leads with his 'weak' hand and the foot on that same side. The 'strong' hand (the one you write with) is kept in reserve for the knockout punch. This is probably as good as anything. Fend off an opponent attempting to grapple using your 'weak' hand. All boxers end up as good with their 'weak' as their 'strong' hand.

Something a boxer does not need to think about: you should keep your hips twisted a little side-on to your opponent to protect your wedding tackle. This little tip will stop a kick or knee to the crotch better than anything. Keep your knees bent all the time as locked knees can be easily broken with a kick or stamp.

If you are up close and possibly grappling, you should always have your head dipped forward a little so a headbutt against you will hit your forehead rather than your nose. This hurts you less and the other guy more than if he connects with your nose.

## HOW TO ATTACK A MAN

This is easy to say but it takes a great deal of practice to perfect the art. The only reliable way to put a man down quickly and quietly – and this can be learned by anyone – is to hit them on the side of the jaw with your fist. There are lots of other ways, and a mate of mine, who is a Tai Chi master, can reach in slow motion through any guard you put up and touch you on the neck so you turn off like a light. He has done it to me and I couldn't stop him. I don't know how it works but I suspect he does something to your mind so you can't move to stop him.

Getting close enough to punch a man properly may mean taking a little bruising, depending on the situation, but you can also use a feint or apparently drunken stumble to get near to your target. Turn your weak side to him and tuck your chin down to protect it. Hold up your weak hand to protect your face. Get up close, head down so he doesn't see your eyes or your mouth. Everyone licks their lips before punching. Did you know that? Bring your best hand from your hip, with the elbow bent at almost a right angle to connect with the point of his jaw from the side. He will go down as if shot.

This may sound very simple but I have used this trick many hundreds of times and it never fails.

The only way to get good at this is to put yourself in front of a punchbag and hit it for hours. This is good for you anyway. When you punch, keep the hand relaxed until it is about to make contact as this way it can travel faster. Push off with your back foot and transfer weight to your front foot as you strike. You can also practise stamping your front foot as you jab with your weak hand to get the timing right.

This is not a boxing manual, and I'm not a good enough boxer to write one anyway, so that is all I shall say about punching.

## DEFENCE IS BETTER THAN ATTACK

It is always easier to respond to an attack than to go in cold. This is because when a man attacks you he commits his weight and balance and thought to hitting or kicking you and the momentum of this combination keeps him going in one direction and gives you time to move around the attack and respond.

The vital thing is that you keep the 'fighting distance' sufficient that he cannot hit you or kick you without stepping forward. The time it takes him to do this telegraphs his intention to you – providing you have your eyes open – and gives you time to respond in the most useful manner.

## HEAD-DOWN CHARGE

Sometimes a man will come at you head down and running to try to close the distance between you and get to grips. This tells you straight away that he cannot fight, but if he is a big, strong chap he still may be a problem. There are two ways I will teach you to deal with this.

As he comes close, step to your weak side. Press down on the back of his head with your strong hand to control him and grip his ear with your weak hand. You should aim to compress the main part of his ear flap between your four fingers and palm. Turn away from him, pulling him by the ear, and extend your gripping arm almost straight, but not fully straight as it is easy to get a broken elbow.

From here you can lead him in a circle around you, all the while off balance, with his head down and just in the right place to keep hitting him with your strong hand. This can continue for as long as he can stay on his feet.

Alternatively, step to the side and grab his hair or collar at the back. Pull him forward the way he is coming so he is off balance. With your leg which is away from his body step forward and place your foot between his feet in such a way that as you move forward your weight goes on to your front foot and your shin pushes his rear leg behind his leading leg. As he tries to take his next step, he will go down in a heap and if you pulled hard enough he may damage himself. If possible you should aim him into a wall.

## GRABBING YOUR COLLAR OR THROAT

If someone manages to get close and grab your collar, the best response depends on how well they have a grip and how strong they look relative to you. There are two potential responses.

Reach up between his arms and grip them around the inside of the elbow. Press out, down and towards you to bring his face forward to meet your forehead.

Alternatively, reach inside his hands from underneath and take a firm grip on his thumbs with your fingers on top and thumbs underneath. Twist his thumbs down and out, bringing his face down to meet your forehead or rising knee.

If your opponent manages to get a firm grip on you and his position stops you using the above, tripping him will often cause him to release you as he falls.

To do what is called outside reaping, turn your right side to your man, then push and pull back, bringing him with you. This draws his weight on to his right foot. Step around his leg with your right foot and push to your front, his right, and roll him off balance over your right leg. Stamp to finish.

For inside reaping, push him so he responds with a push back. Notice which leg he is leading with, then place your same-side leg between his legs and hook around his leading leg with your knee area. Pull his knee towards you and push his upper body away and to the side of his leading leg. He will go over. If he hangs on, follow him and push his head to the floor.

## KICKING ATTACK

Someone only tries to kick you when you are face-on and standing if they think they are close enough to reach you. You should take a small step backwards to avoid their boot contacting with your bollocks. Left alone, the foot will come either straight up in front of you or at a slight angle. Probably the guy will fall over as he was expecting his boot to be stopped by your tender bits. There are several things we can do which are all a lot better than letting him fall over.

Step back and as his foot comes up catch his heel with both hands and lift hard. Release and he will probably do a partial back flip, coming down on the back of his head.

Step back and catch his heel but as you lift it step forward while maintaining the grip and kick him firmly in the bollocks. Repeat as required.

Rather than this, you might wish to break his leg. As his foot comes up to the top of its swing, place one hand on the toe of his boot and the other under the heel. Move back a little further and twist the foot so the toe goes towards the side of his body – across his body. As his whole body starts to follow this move to avoid a twisted knee, pull back so the leg is straight, then twist the other way to break the knee. You may at this point wish to move forward placing the sole of his boot against the inside of your upper arm and getting your shoulder weight behind the twist.

Because any of these moves could be done to you, it is rarely a good idea to kick and never above waist height.

## PUNCHING ATTACK

A boxer will usually punch straight at you as this is fast and hard to avoid other than by keeping your fighting distance, which is what other boxers do. This ends up in a stalemate or boxing match on the street, which is fine if you like an audience and he has no friends to get around behind you. A non-boxer will always swing a punch at you rather than jab as this is all he knows. A swinging punch or roundhouse is easy to see coming, dodge and reply to, as we shall see. Assume for the following explanations a right-handed roundhouse punch coming at you.

Rock back enough to dodge the blow, then step forward left foot first. Lift your right hand with the wrist cocked and press the back of your hand against his outside elbow/upper arm area. Push to the right to force him to continue his movement. Step forward with your right foot and place it behind his right leg (as in outside reaping, above). Move your weight forward, then grab him anywhere on the upper body and push him down in such a way that he falls backwards over your right leg. This move prevents him from landing comfortably, so as he goes down his head will probably strike first. Step away to clear his body, then return to stamp on his head or throat.

A firm stamp to a head raised from a hard floor will

fracture the skull. A stamp to the throat will set off a reflex which causes choking and may well be fatal.

If he is too close, or there is something behind you, step inside the blow with your left forearm raised vertically to catch his inside forearm. Pull back when you make contact to bring him off balance, then step in to push him over your right leg and continue as above.

Alternatively, if you can punch, catch his arm as above, then pull him on to your best right-handed haymaker to the chin.

If you want to hold him for some reason, lift your left arm to catch the blow but then raise it higher, out and down the outside of his arm to catch his arm under your armpit. Apply pressure to his elbow as your arm comes down and press down and in. This makes him spin his face to your right and his back to you as he seeks to avoid a dislocated shoulder. As his back comes towards you, raise his elbow and hang on to his hand to maintain control. Alternatively, step back to drop him on his back and move in to stamp.

## Part Three

# How To Stay Alive When People Want You Dead

You know now how to raise the odds on your getting out of all sorts of scrapes. Once you are up and away you know how to prevent the enemy catching you again by keeping out of his way or killing him. All you have to worry about now is fixing up any damage you might have taken, finding out which way home is, getting some food inside you and surviving the climate.

Perhaps this isn't as glamorous as a stand-up fight but we all operate better with a good meal inside us and dry boots on our feet. I know I do.

We are going to start off with fixing up any wounds or injuries you may have picked up because that is probably the next most urgent task you have. Then we will look at navigation and signalling for a taxi, followed by getting yourself something to eat and drink, and finally how to find or build a shelter.

The reason I have done it this way is as follows: if you have a hole in you or a lump of shrapnel, you want to deal with that first. Once you have that under control, you should be thinking about which way home is or how to get in touch with base. Only if you can't get yourself home in a day or two do you need to think about getting food. And only if you need to lie up to hide or recover do you need to think about shelter.

# Chapter Twelve

# Medical Aid

It is crucial to be able to fix up yourself and your mates in the event of being shot or otherwise injured and there is no help on the way. It sounds a bit boring right up until you need it.

All kids should be taught first aid at school and some are. But you weren't, were you? Nowadays, they teach kids all sorts of bullshit and don't bother so much with the useful stuff. If you are in the forces, you have probably done some first aid and forgotten it. When you know you are going into action, get yourself on another course or at least read a book on it. You will be surprised how often you need to patch people up when the shit starts flying and people are standing around not knowing what to do. Or worse, wanting to do the wrong thing.

When you come across someone in civilian life who is a little the worse for wear, you don't always know what has happened so you check the airways are clear, check they are breathing OK, check their heart is working and then stop any bleeding. This is done in the order of urgency, because as a rule someone dies of having no air faster than losing a little blood. Or if you live somewhere they are going to sue you for helping perhaps you don't give them a hand. What a sick society!

One evening around seven o'clock I was in the south-west of England and driving over to my fencing club alone. It was a twisting lane with woodland on both sides and pretty dark when I came around a corner to see a car lying across the road on its roof with its wheels still spinning. I put the hazards on and pulled in to take a look. There were four boys of 18 or so at the scene and it looked as though they had been driving a little too quickly for either the road or their ability. Three were milling around in shock and the fourth was sitting on the floor semi-conscious.

Checking him over revealed he had no broken bones or major cuts but a hole in his head about two or three inches across with the brain visible. There had obviously been some sort of impact, probably with the ceiling inside the car. There is little can be done with such an injury on the spot as even if I'd had painkillers, which I didn't, they should not be given to head injuries, and there was next to no bleeding.

His pupils worked in unison so there was probably no major brain injury but I covered the wound with a light cloth to keep the dirt out. Obviously, he couldn't see the wound so I told him I had seen worse cuts shaving and that it felt worse to him than it was. The only other thing I could do was keep him awake, calm and warm, so I did this and stayed for a few minutes until the rescue services arrived.

I'm not telling you this story because it teaches you much about treating injuries and not to make me look like I'm a nice guy, because I'm not. What I want you to take away from this is that you can come across an injury at any time at all and you need to be ready. Even if you don't care much about strangers, it could be a friend, family member or yourself. Learn some first aid.

What we are going to look at here are the sort of wounds, injuries and ailments which you might have to treat on yourself or your mates after a chopper crash or a shooting match or while on the run. In short, these are gunshot and shrapnel wounds, other lacerations, fractures, infections and the shits.

Probably the main difference from what you will normally do medically to an injured mate or yourself stems from the fact that the real medics are not going to be on the spot in ten or fifteen minutes. So you don't just have to keep them from bleeding to death and stick some morphine in them. You have to clean and stitch up the wounds, set the bones and give them an antibiotic by syringe or mouth to stop infection in the wound. What I want you to do tomorrow is go out and find yourself a good first aid book and get a grip on the basics.

The sort of injuries you are going to be dealing with in a survival situation are pretty straightforward, so I shall run through them briefly here and give you the reasons for the actions as we go so that you will perhaps remember them better.

You will be able to treat yourself for some problems and injuries, such as infections or a bit of a scratch that needs sewing up, but most people are not really up to setting their own bones so some things need a mate to help. Use your judgement and hope you have a good mate about when you need one.

## IMMEDIATE ACTION

If there is any way you can call for a real medic, do this or have someone do it ASAP. Then look at the casualty. Very often it will be obvious what is wrong but it is always good to have some system to fall back on.

Airway, Breathing, Circulation: the St John Ambulance people teach this ABC as a way of remembering what to do first when you come across an injured person. It may sound a little simplistic but I think it is a good idea. Most people, civilians in particular, don't encounter injuries every day so they may be a little shocked and something to help the memory is perhaps a good idea to get them going.

If the person is awake and alert, they can probably tell you what is wrong and what happened. If they are screaming they are probably not hurt too badly. If they are unable to talk, consider the following:

Airway: if you come across someone unconscious, first check they *can* breathe by opening their mouth and examining the airway for obstructions such as false teeth, puke or whatever. If there is, clear it out with your fingers. Sometimes a deeply unconscious person's tongue falls back in their throat and blocks the airway. The way to deal with this is to place them in the recovery position, and we will come to that in a moment.

Breathing: then you check that they *are* breathing – it may be obvious or you may have to place your ear to their mouth or even a cold glass if you have one handy. If they are not breathing, you will have to cover their nose and blow into their mouth to inflate the lungs. Allow them to breathe out naturally, then repeat until they start breathing unaided.

Circulation: if blood is gushing out of them, the heart is working. If you can see no serious bleeding, check the heart beat by listening to the chest or placing your fingers on the inside of the wrist or neck to check for pulse. Practise this in advance as it is not as easy as it sounds.

A person can die of blood loss in a matter of seconds if a major artery is severed in the neck, wrist or inside the groin. If a medic is on the way, apply pressure to a bleeding artery to cut down the blood loss until the medic arrives. If no medic is coming, the person is going to die.

When you have the airway clear and breathing started, the heart running and bleeding stopped, place the casualty in the recovery position. This means laid out three-quarters face down – not flat on the face – with the upper leg bent at the knee and the upper arm bent at the elbow. In this position a person's tongue will not fall to block their airway and they have a chance for the body to get its act together while a medic arrives or you decide what to do with them.

In civilian life you should not go any further than this as a medic will always be more skilful than we can ever be.

## BULLET AND SHRAPNEL WOUNDS

Bullets can tear off limbs and the shock wave can rip our guts out, but sometimes they just make holes, like shrapnel does, and we can deal with this. It is just a matter of stopping the bleeding, setting any broken bones and stopping the lungs collapsing if necessary.

## COLLAPSED LUNGS

If someone gets shot in the chest, there is at least an entry hole to let air into their chest cavity. There may be an exit hole too. If the bullet goes through their heart, liver or kidneys, they will die unless you get them to a hospital quickly, so we won't worry about that. If the bullet just goes through the lungs, there is usually little blood but, because lungs take in air by your diaphragm pulling down and 'sucking' them open, if there is a hole in the chest wall or ribcage, there is no suction to open the lungs and they will collapse. The casualty will not be able to breathe. Fortunately, this condition, called a 'sucking wound', for obvious reasons if you see and hear one, is easy to deal with on the spot.

Get a bit of plastic bag and smear blood on it to make an air-tight seal against the skin. Cut back the clothing and place the plastic over the hole – which will be making a gross sucking noise as the wounded person tries to breathe – and fasten it in place. Then turn the casualty over into the recovery position with the wound as low as possible. This will allow it to drain and should give the person the use of one lung to keep them going for a while. Again, if a lift to hospital is not available, they are going to die.

Once in Mozambique I was asked to fix up a sucking wound caused by an M16 rifle on a terrorist who was wanted alive for interrogation. He was doing quite well after my treatment but the fire-fight was still warm and the choppers coming in to collect him and our wounded were getting shot to pieces so, as he was not as important as our casualties, he was shot rather than being left to die slowly.

## GUT SHOT

If anyone gets shot in the belly, they have come really unstuck. I have seen one or two and it seems the most painful thing you wouldn't want to experience. They either writhe about digging their nails in the ground or lie there trying to stuff their guts back in their bellies. Worse than the pain, the bullet travelling through the intestine mixes your shit with your bloodstream and causes massive infection which is only treatable in a hospital. If a casevac is coming, give morphine and cover any exposed guts with a cloth. Do not try to stick them back in as this will take in more infection. If a medic is not on the way, give the casualty a hefty dose of morphine to keep them comfortable for the half-hour it will take them to die.

## CUTS AND BLOOD LOSS

If someone is losing blood from a cut or other wound, place a wad of cloth on it and apply pressure to give the clotting agent in the blood time to block the hole. If the hole or tear is larger than about half an inch, you should sew it up with a suture kit. This is just a hooked needle on the end of some thread-type material. Get hold of the needle with some tweezers if you have them and sew the flesh back together. This is very easy to do and helps stop the bleeding amazingly well. It is not very painful and does not need an anaesthetic, although they might thank you for a shot of morphine if it is in a tender spot. After bleeding has occurred always treat for infection.

If someone has lost a lot of blood, they are going to feel 'spacey' and weak and will also be suffering from clinical shock. The best way to treat this is get a saline drip into them. You will need to be shown how to do it by a medic but it is very easy. The needle bit goes into a vein and the bag full of salt water and vitamins or whatever is raised to let it run in. You set the drip rate in the little viewing window to whatever it says on the box. In South Africa, we used to give each other a drip after a night's heavy drinking to help rehydrate the brain. It is an excellent hangover cure.

## BROKEN BONES

All broken bones are called fractures by the medical profession. There are many types of fracture but for our purposes we will consider a clean break where the bone has just snapped, a compound fracture where the bone is either sticking out of the flesh or a wound leads down to it, and a greenstick where the bone is shattered. A clean break can be set by easing the bone ends back into position and splinting the limb so that it heals straight. The bone should be as good as new in six to eight weeks. The other types of break need professional help, so if it is not available the casualty is going to suffer and eventually die. Broken ribs are just sore and heal by themselves – but better if you don't laugh. Breaks to the hands you can put up with. Broken arms are not going to stop you walking but a broken leg can be a death sentence.

Be careful using your fists on someone's head as the

hard bone around the eye socket can easily break the bones in your hands. If you hit them hard enough, the bones in the back of your hand will break. Once I came back to camp from a night on the piss and a South African officer was asleep in my tent and in my bed. There were plenty of tents with mattresses so I let it go and slept elsewhere. The next day he had disappeared and the bed clothes were lying around the tent. It was clear he was taking the Michael so I went to see him and gave him a thorough beating. Perhaps I was a little excited and wanted to make a mess of his face so he would remember me. Whatever, I broke the bones in the back of my hands and they never set right – leaving lumps to this day – but it makes no odds to the use of the hands.

## INFECTION

You can get infection from any cut and sometimes without any noticeable damage at all. Infections happen easily and severely in hot countries and even more so in hot, wet places like jungles. If you cut yourself, always treat for infection to avoid the pain, swelling and fever which will follow. Don't think this is just for your comfort either – an untreated infection can lead in short order to death.

You should be able to get antibiotic pills to treat infection and there are very many types, some of which work better for some things than others. The sort of thing you want is called a Broad Spectrum Antibiotic which, as it says on the tin, deals with most things. The thing about antibiotics is that you need to take a full course of a week (or whatever is specified) to make sure the infection does not come back – even if it seems to have entirely cleared. This is because you need to keep the level of antibiotic in your bloodstream above a certain concentration for a certain length of time to stop the bugs breeding again.

Infection can also be treated by injection but this is usually reserved for giving the bugs a hard knock in hospital or similar. Sometimes an injection is given to bring the concentration of antibiotic up quickly in an emergency and then the remainder of the course is given orally.

## THE SHITS

In many warm countries, you can pick up bugs which give you the shits. These may be nameless little sods which don't amount to much aside from this effect, or they may be something more serious like dysentery caught from a polluted water supply. The best way to avoid the shits is to sterilise all your water and don't eat food which has not been cooked properly. This is, of course, often impossible.

The main problem with having the squirts is that you pass so much water out of your body that you can become dehydrated more than is good for you. There are pills which should stop the shits and until it is fixed make sure you drink loads of water or you will get weak and dizzy.

## Chapter Thirteen

# Navigation And Signalling For Rescue

I'm now going to show you how to find your way home across country over any terrain – or get someone to come and fetch you.

Before you go on any operation, you should have the general map of the area committed to memory. If you don't, you deserve to get lost. Main towns, roads, and rivers if any, and most of all where your base or the border is.

Much of the time your situation will mean you know roughly where you are – like you have been out on patrol – and there is no problem. But if you have just come down in a chopper or broken out of a prison you don't know where you are and things get more interesting. At worst you will have a general idea of the layout of the country where you are operating but not actually know where you are within this map as the chopper could have come down anywhere within several grid squares or you could have been transported some distance to a prison or holding area.

There are more demoralising things than following on foot a road that heads off to a point on the horizon but it is certainly up there. Obviously, if you have found a road and it is going your way, you have a number of alternatives according to your situation: you could thumb a lift, stop a car with a shot at the windscreen and take it or you could simply follow the road on foot.

If you have decided to walk and the ground is wooded, you need to be able to get into the woods at short notice to hide from travellers. If the ground is open desert, I'm afraid you need to keep your eyes open and if a vehicle approaches get away from the road and lie down. Of course, it will be night, so there will be headlights to warn you.

## CALLING THE TAXI COMPANY

By far the easiest way to get home is to call for a chopper. The flyboys just turn up and run you home to the girls and the beer. If you were on patrol and your team has just taken a hiding, you may well have the necessary equipment to call for someone to come and get you. Even if you don't, there is a good chance your people will be looking for you and have a good idea where you are. If your own chopper has come down, the same applies, but if you have just broken out of somewhere you may be short of communications equipment and perhaps no one knows where you are.

Call for a ride as quickly as possible after the event, if you can, so you don't have to spend longer than necessary trying to stay alive. In many situations, if you have a radio, a satellite phone or a mobile phone that is working, you can simply call a chopper.

Signalling for rescue is where it all comes down to the kit you have organised. As you are one of the good guys, there are going to be all manner of people back at base who are missing you and wondering where you are. Just like your mum really. In many cases, such as bandit country within a country you are pacifying, there will be help on the way before the wreck you stepped out of is cold. But it might still help them get to you more quickly if you have some sort of electronic gizmo to give them your position.

If you are in a reasonably 'friendly' country, say on a peacekeeping mission, you might have a mobile phone that works. They do need boosters to transmit voice but as long as it is switched on there are ways for our guys to track you down to within a few feet and come to collect you. At least there are if they have an electronics surveillance aircraft in the area – an AWACS or similar. If you have had to run and hide from a crash or a gunfight this will be quite reassuring.

A step up from this is a radio distress beacon such as are used by yachtsmen and some parts of the military. Switch it on and all the Friendlies will home in on you like wasps to jam. I don't know if you can get one issued but I bet you could get hold of one if you tried.

As I write, a satellite phone is still a bit of a beast to lug about but mobile phones were the size of a car battery when they first came out so there is hope for satellite phones to get a lot smaller. A satellite phone talks straight to the satellite relay rather than a booster station and therefore works more or less anywhere. Call for a taxi.

To call for a ride, all you need to do is tell anyone friendly that is listening who you are, what the situation is and where to find you. Any operator who picks up the call will pass it on as a priority message. If your people know you are in trouble, they may be monitoring all radio traffic in the area and pick up your call for help straight away or your emergency beacon.

But if you are in a country which is officially unfriendly to your own the cavalry may not be able to come and get you. This means you will have to get to where you can get a ride under your own steam. We'll look at this in a moment.

Suppose you have got in touch with base and they are going to send a chopper for you. What else do you need to do other than sit about taking in the view and trying to stop the locals hacking pieces off you? Your own people will be able to pick up your position from your signal – whatever means of communication you are using. This will tell them where you are within a few metres but it does not tell them the situation. If you have more than a beacon running, so you have two-way comms, you should tell them to meet you somewhere which is open and safe for them to land without fear of ambush.

Do be aware that unfriendly ears may be listening to your chat, so there is the possibility of an ambush for the chopper or someone nasty homing in on you too. Probably the safest way to go in many cases is to give the chopper a grid reference and/or a feature on the ground to meet you at. Then switch off your comms so you can make your way to this at the right time and be reasonably sure no one else will be waiting there.

The safest place for a chopper to land is in the open, flat desert but finding a spot like this is down entirely to luck as you don't get a choice as to where you have your nightmare. Try to pick somewhere which is flat for ease of landing and not overshadowed by rocks or hills where an ambush could easily be arranged. When the taxi does arrive, it may, if the situation warrants it, have one or more escorts ready to plaster the area around you with fire while you are collected.

If your situation allows you to be fairly open about your position because the country is empty and there are no unfriendly aircraft, mark out a large 'H' on the ground as the universal signal for a chopper to land. Failing this, you could light a fire and have a pile of wet leaves to put on it to make smoke as the rescue team comes in sight.

But what do you do if no one is coming for you? If you are unable to make contact with your base in a country where you have been on normal operations, eventually they will come looking for you and have a good idea where you might be. All you have to do is stay alive long enough for them to find you.

In a country where you have been up to something sneaky or naughty, you may have to make it under your own steam to a friendly border or the coast. At the border, you should be able to get a message to your own people and at the coast they are likely to come and collect you by small boat or submarine if you are worth the trouble.

· If you are on the shore and wanting a lift from a boat or sub, they will be looking for you or they would not be there. If you have nothing else, a flashlight to signal SOS or your unit call sign is as good as anything. Learn enough Morse code to do this. SOS is just three dots, three dashes, three dots, so doing short and long flashes on a torch to transmit this is easy enough. Make sure you don't signal the bad guys.

Taking either of these options can mean finding your way across hundreds of miles of country full of unfriendly natives. We have already looked at dealing with the locals, and we will look at food and other details shortly, but now you need to learn how to find your way to safety.

## MAP READING AND NAVIGATION

So there is no taxi coming and you are going to have to make your own way home, or at least to the border or seaside. To do that, you will need to know roughly how the land lies, where you are and how far it is. Knowing the right direction to walk is good too.

I suppose it is possible you have a GPS box (Global Positioning Service) and no phone, such is the magic of technology today, and in that case you will know exactly where you are. If you have the deluxe model, it might even show you a map of where you are and have a built-in bleeper to tell your friends where you are. With such a clever bit of kit you just follow the arrows like using a satnav. Failing that, you will have to do it the old-fashioned way, and I'll tell you how to do that now.

For the sort of navigation we are talking about here, it helps to have a map but you can do a surprising amount even if that map is in your head! If in your mind's eye you can picture where you are and you know that there is a road to the South of you which heads off East to the coast, you have a good idea which way to go.

The trouble comes when you have to avoid towns or find bridges and tricky little things like that. It's best if I tell you how it should be done with a map and little else, then you can mix and match what you do have to suit.

## FINDING NORTH AND SOUTH

As a basic rule, you start off by finding where North is so you can 'get your bearings'. This means orientate your mental or physical map to the lie of the land. If you know 'this way is North', you can point the North, the top, of the map that way so that it lies the same way as the land. This is called orienting your map. Then, as you look at the map, away from you is North, towards you is South and so on.

There are several ways of finding North without equipment but the easiest is a compass and there is no excuse for not having a compass the size of a thumbnail in your survival kit. If you are a bit more organised, there is the trusty compass made by Silva, which is about the size of a flattened cigarette packet. A tiny compass will just tell you where North is so you know roughly which way to go. A Silva compass will also let you take bearings to and from features on the ground and also on a map. We will look at bearings in a moment. A better compass, such as the prismatic, actually has sights to take accurate bearings but is probably more than you really need on a survival trip.

If you don't have a compass, there are two easy ways of finding North. One for daylight, using a watch that has hands, and one for the night, using the stars. In daylight, North of the equator, hold your watch level and point the hour hand at the sun. The position halfway between the hour hand and 12 o'clock on the dial is now pointing due South. If it is eight o'clock in the morning and you point the hour hand at the sun, South will be in the direction of the ten o'clock marker. If it is four o'clock in the afternoon and you do the same, South will be in the direction of the two o'clock marker.

South of the equator, everything is reversed. Point the 12 o'clock marker at the sun and the point halfway between this and the hour hand will indicate North. This all may sound more complicated than it actually is, but try it now and you will find it works a treat.

If you cannot easily see the sun, stand a stick upright and you should be able to make out the sun's position from the shadow it casts and then work out the rest.

In the Northern hemisphere, you need a clear dark sky and to look for this formation of stars. The thing to remember is that as the earth rotates every night the Big Dipper rotates around the North Star. [ill??]

The Southern hemisphere is a little more tricky as there is no actual star marking South. You need to find the Southern Cross and estimate South as shown in the diagram. Again, remember the constellation rotates around the Southern point in the sky.

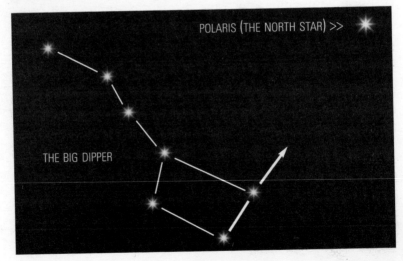

POLARIS (THE NORTH STAR) >>

THE BIG DIPPER

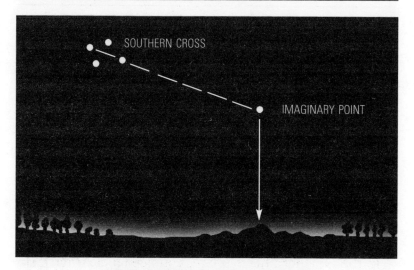

## FINDING YOUR POSITION

If you want to know where you are, you can always look at the road signs but, if these are in Arabic, how good is your grasp of the language? Roads, however, are marked on maps, being the principal feature, and, if you can get a back-bearing on just one feature, then where the line crosses the road is where you are. I can hear you muttering, 'What's a bloody back-bearing?'

Listen up while I explain the basics of how to use a compass for those who were never taught – and also for those too stupid to listen when told about this vital soldiering skill. There are many other things you can do with a compass besides finding North. Among them is finding out where you are with a fair degree of accuracy. This is called a resection. If you can see mountains or the lights of a city or some other feature which will be marked on a map, take a bearing on it. To take a bearing you point the compass body arrow at the feature and then line up the arrows on the compass dial with the needle. Then you read off the figures from the dial around the arrows.

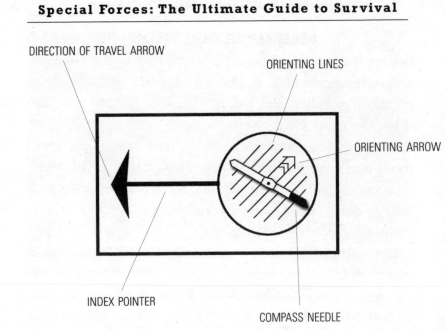

DIRECTION OF TRAVEL ARROW

ORIENTING LINES

ORIENTING ARROW

INDEX POINTER

COMPASS NEEDLE

You then turn the bearing, which is from you to the feature, into a back-bearing, which is from the feature to you, by adding 180 degrees (i.e. the distance between North and South). If you draw, or imagine, a line on the map at the back-bearing angle from the feature, it must cross the point where you are taking the measurement from. You are actually along that line somewhere.

Another feature, if possible at a wide angle from the first to achieve better accuracy, with another back-bearing gives another line and where they cross is where you are sitting. All soldiers should have been taught how to do a resection at birth.

If you are unable to find two features suitable for a resection you can do the same thing with a road or a river, if you are on either, plus one feature. Take a bearing, turn it into a back-bearing, then draw it on the map. Where it crosses the road or river is where you are.

## MAGNETIC VARIATION

Believe it or not, the Magnetic North Pole wanders about a few fractions of a degree every year. And not in a regular way either. This means Magnetic North on a map is not the exact Grid North where the up and down grid lines point. The older the map, the greater the difference too. I don't want to get too complicated here as this level of accuracy is not really needed for what we are doing but I don't want some smart-arse saying I never mentioned it.

If you need to be accurate, read off the magnetic variation as it says on the map legend. Work out how old the map is and tot up the amount the variation has changed since the map was published. This gives you a current magnetic variation to change your magnetic bearings from the compass into the grid bearings you should plot on to the map. Remember the rhyme 'Mag to Grid get rid', then to change a magnetic bearing from your compass to a grid bearing on your map subtract the magnetic variation. It will only be a few degrees so you can probably forget about it now.

## SETTING YOUR COURSE

Now you know where you are, and presumably where you want to get to, you need to work out a route, then set off in that direction. In principle, you lay the compass on the map so the edge lies along the line between where you are and where you want to get to. Then you turn the dial until the North points to North on the map. Change this from Grid to Mag if you are fussy and when you line up the compass with Magnetic North the direction arrow will point in the direction you want to be going. Easy.

When it comes to walking on a compass bearing it is best to sight along the compass to a feature on the horizon and head for that. It is both easier than holding the compass out in front of you all the time and it stops you crabbing off to the side as you go.

## AIM OFF FOR A BRIDGE

If you need to find a specific point on a known line, such as a bridge over a river or a house on a road, you do not work out your bearing and head straight for it. The reason is that you will very often miss the target and not be sure which way to turn when you reach the road or river.

The thing to do in this case is always head off a little to one side, say right, or as you think best in the circumstances, so that when you do arrive at the road or river you know for sure that you only have to turn, say left, and you will hit the target.

## JUDGING DISTANCE TRAVELLED

Before you get yourself lost, it is a good idea to practise timing yourself walking over known distances so that when you are moving across country you can estimate how far you have covered. The speed you make will vary quite a lot depending on your condition and the type of country but with practice you can get quite accurate. Then, when you have been walking two hours, you will know you have covered eight clicks or whatever. You will also be able to estimate how long it will take you to get to various points and this can be important when you don't want to be caught out in the open during daylight or want to make your water last.

## SO WHERE DOES THAT LEAVE YOU?

When you know where you are and where you have to get to, you know how far it is. If you have a map, you know what the country is like and what obstacles there may be along the way, like swamps, rivers, mountains, cities and so on. If you consider this and take into account how fast you can march over that distance and make a decision on whether it is better to travel by day or by night, you will have a good idea of how long it is going to take you to get there. And knowing that will tell you how thirsty and hungry you are going to get.

This is where you have to start thinking about getting yourself some water and possibly food.

## Chapter Fourteen

# Getting Food And Water: Don't Eat The Bugs

You need to know how to live off the land if you have to, live off the locals if you can, and when to live off your body fat.

The chances are that you are not going to be stuck out on your lonesome for very long. A chopper could be with you in minutes or hours and in a similar time you could run back to base camp from most other situations. It is only if you have come really short, like being a long way behind enemy lines or up in the mountains in bad weather, that you will need to think about food and water. Still, this wouldn't be a proper survival book if I didn't show you how to boil a few mushrooms, would it? What I am going to do is tell you enough to keep body and soul together if you have to collect wild food and then tell you how to feed yourself properly.

### WHERE YOU ARE STARTING FROM

Unless you have just escaped from somewhere, or lost all your kit somehow, you ought to be carrying at least a couple of water bottles on your belt. Even if you were on a foot patrol and lost your pack with your reserves, you should still have your belt kit. It should be an absolute golden rule that in a combat zone you carry on your belt at all times a couple of bottles of water, 100 rounds of ammunition, a knife, a field dressing, basic medical equipment and a tiny survival kit. This kit will include water containers and water-sterilisation pills, among other things. Your knife should be light enough to fight with and heavy enough to cut wooden branches. A saw on the back of this is not a bad thing.

## WATER

First of all, we need to look at the water situation. You don't need to think about food unless you are going to be out for more than about four days but if you are short of water for more than a day or so you will get uncomfortable. A few days and you will not be able to march. A little longer and you will die.

In a temperate climate, there is usually lots of water around but not in the mountains or semi-desert of, say, Afghanistan. But it isn't just finding water that is the problem. Finding water is obviously better than not, but if you cannot carry it you might find yourself stuck at a water hole until someone finds you or you die of hunger. And if someone finds you that could be good or bad, depending.

So you will always carry water bottles on your belt, won't you? Not just for the water in them but for carrying refills. And if you escape from somewhere and it looks like you will be out for a while the first thing you need to do is find yourself some way of carrying water.

This might be plastic bottles, plastic bags or whatever. Make a sling with some cord as water gets heavy. If you are going somewhere you expect might be tricky, then in every decent outdoors shop there are some really clever variations on the old plastic bag for carrying water which usefully fold flat when empty.

As long as you have some way of carrying it, you won't normally have trouble finding water and moving on. Take the cleanest water you can see from a stream if you can, or a well if you have to. Then add the sterilisation tablets in the ratio on the box. This will make it safe to drink, if not appetising. Don't worry, when you are thirsty, just like when you are hungry, your perception of what is acceptable changes in a spooky sort of way, so if the water smells bad or looks yellow you can just put up with it. The locals can probably drink this stuff and thrive on it but if you do you will go down with the shits or worse. Boil it if you don't have the pills and if you can't boil it only drink it if it is from a clear running source like a mountain stream – unless you have to.

If you are in the mountains, snow can be melted against your body in a bag. If there is no snow, look for a swampy area in a hollow and dig there until the hollow fills. In dry areas things are more tricky but dry river beds mark where the water table is closest to the surface. If you are desperate you might try digging there but it could be a long way down.

Before you use all your energy on digging, you should be drinking your own piss as your body can use it a couple of times over.

Where there are grazing animals there will be a water supply, even if it has people attached to it, as the animals have to have water pretty much daily. In the absence of anything useful, follow a road or track and it will eventually lead to a house. They will have water but you should be careful. Buy water and the locals will all know about you within hours. Kill the occupants of the house and you have a little more time but the best idea by far is to steal clean water from barns, animal troughs or similar.

If you are really stuck, you can slit the throat of an animal or human and drink the blood. This will seem a better idea when you have been without water for a couple of days under the sun.

There is a lot of bullshit talked about needing to keep yourself hydrated and you see people walking about town sipping from bottles all day. This is like a child with its security blanket. If water is short, the weather is hot and you are travelling in the day for some reason, do not drink or it will come straight out in sweat. If you must travel by day, have a good drink at night when you have settled down and a small one in the morning well before you set off. I have done this for weeks on end in hot countries and it works well enough and saves carrying huge amounts of water. I didn't say it was comfortable, mind.

The best thing is not to get yourself into this sort of mess about water. In hot countries, travel at night if you possibly can, so you sweat less, and lie up during the day. Top up your water supplies whenever you come across water and plan your route with water in mind if water is an issue where you are. This may mean hopping from village to village or it might mean river to river.

## NO FOOD

You are good for about four days without eating and can quite easily function for this sort of period without any serious loss of efficiency. If you are carrying concentrates on your belt or even K pills – sugar pills for energy – you can keep going for a couple of weeks without trouble. You do need to ration your supplies carefully, though, as you don't actually need a great many calories to keep marching and they can seem very tasty when you are hungry. The human body can do with a lot less than you might think.

If you expect from your route plan to get home or meet your ride in less than four days, you should not think about stealing or catching food. Every extra hour you spend in bandit country looking for the canteen adds to the risk of your being caught, so time is always an issue to be weighed against the advantages of stopping to rest, recover from injury, find food or stop for any other reason. It is simply not worth the delay of hunting or the risk of stealing food if you can do without. Anyway, being hungry will motivate you to walk faster.

## STEALING FOOD

It is possible to collect mushrooms and various seeds but there won't be any there when you need them and despite what they say in all the survival books they are hardly worth eating as there is so little energy in them.

For the energy to march, you are best with carbohydrates such as potatoes and bread but these do not grow wild. The next best thing is meat of any kind, which does grow wild but resents being eaten and takes some catching. Another advantage of meat is that it is always in season. You might be used to collecting fancy fruit and vegetables from the supermarket but they don't grow all year round in the one country, you know.

Given that there are no vegetables worth having in the sticks, and the meat runs away when you want it, the easiest way to get food if you really need it is to steal it from a farmer's field or barn. If you are lucky with the season there might be maize, potatoes, yams, carrots or other high-carbohydrate foods which you can just take from a field without too much risk, but it's quite likely there won't be any. But there just might be a store of potatoes or similar in a clamp or barn, so bear this in mind. Taking everything into consideration, the best available source of food is meat from a domesticated animal. And this you have to steal as buying one tells everyone where you are.

There is a risk of being caught in the act by the owners but you won't be doing it unless you have to, will you? Go for a small animal you can carry, such as a goat. There will not be pigs in Muslim countries but in any event pigs scream when hurt, are hard to kill and are very heavy. Chickens, ducks and geese are plentiful in many areas but they all make a real racket if you try to do one of their buddies harm. Come to think of it, they make a racket even if you don't. Goats and sheep are excellent from the point of view of killing, preparing and eating.

Approach during the late evening after the locals are in bed and make friendly noises. The animals, particularly milking goats, will be used to being handled, after all. If it is at all possible without waking anyone, lead the goat away with you so the farmer will think it may have wandered off.

Slide your knife into the side of the neck near the neck

bone with the blade pointing down. Immediately it is in, pull the knife down to sever the carotid artery and nerves, just like killing a human. The goat will go down silently as if poleaxed but there will be a lot of blood squirting around. This will alert the owner to a missing animal and your presence the next morning if you had to do it on the spot.

If you were going to be staying out for a while, you would hang the carcass from a branch by its back legs while you cut around the ankles and neck and up to the belly to take off the skin. Next you would slice open the skin of the belly, taking care not to burst the intestines and allow the guts and offal to drop on the floor. Take off the head and the remainder is all meat on the bone, fit for a *braaivleis* (roasted meat, or barbecue) as the Afrikaners say. The heart and liver are very, very good for you, as we were taught in the Paras when being obliged to eat them raw and steaming from the freshly killed animal.

If you find yourself in a warm, sunny place with a lot of meat to save, cut it into bootlace-thin strips and hang it over branches and bushes in the sun to make biltong (or jerky in the USA). If you are really on the ball, you will have some salt to add at this stage because meat, raw or cooked, is a whole lot better with salt. As it is you are probably going to be travelling light, so cut off a rear leg or haunch where it joins the body and this will keep you going for some time. It will certainly last a few days without going too bad.

## FINDING FOOD

You can actually eat almost anything green, but there is very little energy in any plant you are likely to find growing wild. Human digestive systems are not made to extract the nutrient from green vegetables eaten raw anyway, so if you are reduced to eating vegetables things must be pretty bad and if possible you should cook them. See below.

Before eating any plant you are not sure of, chew a little piece and hold the wad under your tongue for a minute. If it tastes bitter, spit it out as it is probably poisonous.

The easiest things to find and eat are fungus and nettles. Of all the plants commonly available, nettles are among the best, so if they are about give them a try. Boiled, they are better than most commercial greens in my opinion.

If you are by the sea, you should look for shellfish as these are highly nutritious and, being slow, easy to catch. They are better cooked but can be eaten raw. The same applies to rivers, where you may find freshwater mussels and crayfish. Probably the easiest 'meat' of all to catch is fish – just a baited hook and line in most rivers and ponds will pull up something.

In most places there are lots of insects and the way to look at these is as land shellfish. Grubs and similar are the best for nutrition and go down better if you cook them in a stew of plants.

If you have to live off the land, go for a meat dish every time as this is concentrated calories and almost never poisonous when fresh. You can eat pretty much any animal. When we were young, my mate, the author Yves Debay, used to eat the most disgusting things in front of delicate soldiers just to make them throw up, but animals which eat grass are most appealing. Mice, lizard, snakes (which taste just like chicken), crocodile, birds of all kinds, rabbits and other small critters are favourite if they live where you find yourself. The trick, of course, is catching them.

One time in the Zambezi Valley, Yves had a puff adder creep into his sleeping bag. They have no taste, you know. He calmly killed it with his knife, skinned it and ate it. This freaked out the Africans as they have some sort of taboo on eating snakes.

On the same trip, a hippo came out of the water at night, as they do to eat the grass, and as it was mowing its way around it got a tusk caught in Yves's sleeping bag – while he was still in it. Of course, it ran off with him still in his bag dragging behind it. Talk about laugh! If you were wondering why there was no sentry, it was because, when you have a very small patrol, in many cases, it is better to all sleep in a cross formation than miss enough sleep to mount a guard.

You can take eggs out of birds' nests at the right time of year. In warm countries, this may be a long season. Birds take more catching but you can do it with a little bait and a hook and line.

Rabbits and similar are best caught with a snare. Look for a track which something trots along and set a lasso of wire hanging from a firm branch. Some poor critter will come along at night and get itself caught if you are lucky. Kill it with a club, skin and eat.

## COOKING

Like I said, there is almost no available energy in most green plants when raw. There is little enough when cooked, but as a last resort you can cook any green plant you can find and the cooking process breaks down the cellulose cells and allows your digestive system to get at the goodness, such as it is.

You can also cook almost any fungus which is not

brightly coloured like the red ones with white spots in kiddies' cartoons. Most wild things which are brightly coloured are dangerous and warning you. Only take and eat fungus in an emergency, not for practice, as in most temperate countries there are hundreds and you can't learn them all. Most of them are safe but a few will make you ill and one or two will kill you. Bracket fungus, which grows out from the sides of trees like a shelf, is not poisonous and takes on the flavour of any food you cook it with so that is nice if you have a stew of maggots.

Your body can get some of the nutrient out of high-carb plants such as maize and potatoes without your having to cook them, and you can absorb the protein from raw meat so that is good too, but all foods are easier for your body to digest and extract the energy when cooked.

Meat, freshly killed, raw and without salt tastes a lot better when you have been hungry for a few days, so cooking makes it a lot more palatable too. How do you do that?

There are several limitations on your cooking: giving your position away by smoke during the day or light at night, the time it takes to do the job, and both the amount of water required and the cooking equipment you have with you.

If you have the time, pots and water, the easiest way is to boil your vegetables and add small pieces of meat if you have them. This breaks down the plant stuff so you can absorb it and spreads the goodness out of the meat into all the liquid and vegetable matter so your body can use it better. It also makes the whole thing a lot more appetising.

If you don't have water or cooking pots, you can wrap

your food in clay or thick leaves and put them in a hole with heated rocks from the fire. I think this is generally too fancy and slow.

The quickest and most efficient way to prepare your food is to forget about the veg and cut your meat into small pieces or strips and skewer these on sticks over the fire. They only take a minute to cook and go down very well indeed.

## MAKING FIRE

Like so many other things, fire is a trade-off of risk against benefit and there is no clear answer much of the time. As I said above, light a fire in the day and the smoke will tell people where you are. Light one at night and the light will show for miles unless you are very careful.

On balance, you are probably only sensible to light a fire at night. To hide a fire at night, it must not only be in a hole or have a light-proof barrier around it to stop direct light but it must also be set up in such a way that there are no branches or whatever above to reflect the light to any viewer. Try this at night and you will see that a cigarette is visible for a couple of hundred yards even before you suck on it and a fire can be seen for miles. Worse, a face looking over a hidden fire is lit up for a very long way.

The only times you need to light a fire are to cook vegetables when you are desperate for any food, or to warm yourself or dry your clothes in a cold climate. Everything else is a luxury which may cost you your life.

Of course, you are going to have waxed, waterproof matches in your kit, aren't you? Unless you escaped from somewhere. So how do you light a fire without matches?

The amusing thing is that the easiest way to light a fire is to use sunlight and a magnifying glass. It takes only a few moments to focus the heat from a magnifying glass on to some tinder and get it smoking then blow it into a flame. Trouble is you don't want it in the day, do you? So what you need to do is make a taper with some sort of cord which will smoulder like a wick and keep this until dark, when a good blow will start your fire.

If you are short of tinder, you can bet everything will be damp. Shavings from dry wood are best but you will just have to find what you can.

In the absence of matches or a magnifying glass, you can get a fire going by making a small bow and wrapping the bowstring around a straight stick. Make a top and bottom holder for the stick and spin it backwards and forwards with the bow while applying pressure to the top holder. Very quickly the friction at the top and bottom of the stick will make a little smoke. Add tinder and keep going until you have a glow, then blow to flame.

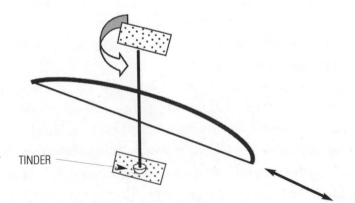

TINDER

You will see now that everything I have told you about eating and drinking is indeed a trade-off: risk against benefit. You either eat well and take risks or starve and stay safe. The only one to make that decision is you on the spot.

# Chapter Fifteen

# Climate And Country

L et's consider how you live and function while on the run in a harsh climate. You are already going to be operating in the general area of the world where you will get into trouble so you ought to be dressed for the occasion. This is not rocket science: if it is cold you want warm clothing and if it is warm you want protection from the sun. You can make life after a disaster a whole lot more comfortable for yourself if you go out well prepared: plastic sheeting, sleeping bag and that sort of thing. See Appendix: Your Survival Kit for details of what you may need.

About the only time you have an excuse for not dressing for the occasion is if you are flying over mountains. It is amazing how cold it gets at only a few thousand feet of altitude and you can test this for yourself by driving up a road into some handy mountains in a car with an outside temperature sensor. Mountains don't have snow on top because God likes the scenery: they have snow because they get bloody cold. So, if you come down in the mountains, it is going to be a hell of a lot colder than it was in the valleys. You may consider, in such a situation, that a brisk walk downhill has a lot to offer as a survival strategy.

When you are in a cold climate, the main problem is not the actual cold but the wind and wet, which make the low temperature affect your body a lot more. I have been on tank exercises in northern Germany where it was 30 below and your fingers would stick to any bare metal because of the way it conducts the heat away. But it didn't actually feel so cold when there was no wind. Obviously, we had warm coats – those parkas with wire in the hoods to keep the snow and wind off your face – but out of the wind it was very reasonable.

In those days, the tanks didn't have heaters, and much of a tank exercise, like all soldiering, is spent waiting, so we crew used to lift up the slatted steel covers over the hot 20-litre diesel engine and climb in with a bottle of brandy between us – Asbach Uralt, as I remember. Actually alcohol is bad for you when it's chilly but, hey, young men drink. Thirteen different types of oil and grease went into keeping our tanks running and, as any tanky will tell you, step within 20 feet of a tank and you are covered in oil. Better warm, though.

Many layers of clothing work better at trapping air for insulation than one thick layer and you can adjust the insulation according to whether you are walking or resting, because you don't want to get too warm and start sweating in a cold climate as this can end in tears as the damp freezes. When you are resting, get out of the wind and keep dry if you can. At least if it's raining it isn't so cold.

A very useful piece of kit for cool weather is a light windproof. This must not be plastic as plastic traps the sweat but something that stops the wind is very handy, when worn over a jersey or whatever, for holding the heat in. You can use a close-woven cotton material but there are a number of clever synthetics on the market nowadays which are much better. The first of these was Gore-Tex, patented in 1976. Look in any outdoor or sailing shop for a selection.

The more tired you get, and the hungrier you get, the less heat your body will generate so you will both feel the cold and be in the running to get hypothermia. This is when your body's core temperature drops below a certain point and the chemistry which keeps it running stops working properly. Strangely, hypothermia feels quite nice: you stop shivering and feel drowsy and even warm. Then you go to sleep and die. This is a strong argument for having the right gear, making windproof shelters and not going to sleep cold. The cure for hypothermia is to warm the guy up. This can be done by placing him in a sleeping bag with another man or by wrapping him in a silver blanket to reflect his heat back at him.

Warm climates, oddly enough, can be more of a problem than cold because of the fatigue caused by the heat and the loss of water. If you are from a temperate zone, it will take your body about four months to get used to a hot climate and until this time has gone by you are going to feel constantly tired. I am not sure why it takes so long but I have experienced acclimatisation to heat often enough to be sure it is the case. You are going to feel the heat even more if the climate is humid, and this is probably because the heat is not carried away from your body when the sweat dries. There is little you can do but drink plenty of water until you get used to it.

All the time you are in the sun, wear a hat which covers your ears and neck and, unless you are very dark-skinned, it's best to keep your arms and legs covered too. Sunburned legs are more sore than you might imagine. My African mates think it is really funny to see a Euro get sunburned but they tan too – you can often see the tan lines where a vest has been taken off.

Sunburn is when the skin gets more sun than it can handle and it turns red, then burns. The more melanin you have in your skin the darker your skin is – from Africans with the most proof against the sun to blondes, natural blondes, who burn looking out of the window on a bright day. You can wear sun-block but you will forget and anyway it is for girls to stop wrinkles. If you are out in the sun a lot, get yourself a good hat like an Australian. This should have a broad brim to protect the back of your neck, your ears and your nose. The corks keep the flies off pretty well too.

Sunstroke, on the other hand, is fatal. It is also called heatstroke and the proper name is hyperthermia – the opposite of hypothermia. What happens is that the body absorbs more heat than it can lose by sweating and panting so the core temperature rises. It does not have to go far before you feel sick and dizzy, then you go into a coma and die. It seems to me that getting sun on the back of your neck heats up the blood quicker and brings it on faster, so watch out for that. Sunstroke requires immediate medical attention and if this is not available the best thing you can do is cool the man by dabbing him with water to allow evaporation or, if possible, throwing him in a river.

Friends in the West find my attitude to the sun amusing, but then I am British. The British love the sun as they see it so rarely at home. When the sun comes out, so do the Brits in their droves and lie out anywhere flat to catch the rays. I, on the other hand, keep in the shade. I am very much a warm-weather soldier and prefer any amount of heat to the cold. But I am also very careful about the sun, even though I would pass for a Latin or a light-skinned Indian, and often have.

When I first went to Africa as a very young man, I was given some make-work at an army camp to keep me busy while waiting for selection for the Rhodesian SAS. As I recall, I had to dig some flower beds. I did this on what seemed like an ordinary English summer's afternoon for just a couple of hours but I was stupid enough to take my shirt off. The next day I was covered from the waist up with huge blisters full of liquid. And I mean covered. Selection started a day or two later and I ran for miles with a pack and its straps bursting my blisters and drawing blood from my back and shoulders before I passed out. I know just how stupid it was to get burned like that and I won't do it again. As a mate of mine who is a hotshot businessman once said to me, 'You have to pay to learn.' He meant that, if something hurts you, you remember it. He meant financially but the principle is sound.

One other thing about working in hot climates. I have said this before and will say it again so you remember: you can only carry so much water and it will go in no time if you drink when you want. What I have found to work well, even though it seems to be against every modern rule, is to drink only when you have finished moving for the day. If you drink in a hot climate the water seems to come straight out as sweat. Now maybe not drinking will give you heatstroke or something but I have worked with many men in the Zambezi Valley, where it is very warm at times, and this is what we did. Walk for 12 hours a day and do no more than wet your lips. Save your water for night, when you can keep it in your system. Of course, in an ideal world, you would be lying up by day and travelling by night but the same applies.

## FOOT ROT

I have said this before in this book and many times elsewhere but if your feet are no good you are dead. The best way to get feet to rot, to start the skin, then flesh, falling off the bones, is to keep them damp all the time. Like if you lie in the bath too long. If your feet get damp while they are in your boots the skin will soften and blisters will rub up. This is not nice but you can live with it. If you keep your feet wet for a long while, they get infected with what they called trench foot in the First World War, where many soldiers caught it from living in water-filled trenches. This probably has a fancy name but trench foot works for me. It is a sort of fungus which just rots the flesh off your feet like the worst athlete's foot you would want to see.

In hot climates, there is a good argument for wearing heavy-soled sandals over bare feet on operations as this allows your feet to stay dry.

On all operations, you should be taking care of your feet – washing them every day and applying anti-fungal powder – but when you are on the run this becomes even more important. If your feet are bad while you are in camp, you might get the medic to give you light duties. I would give you a smack round the ear and extra drill. If you get bad feet while you are on the run and out in the sticks, you may not be able to walk and if that happens you will die.

One of the main things which limited the time the SAS and other special forces could spend in the jungles of Malaya and elsewhere was how long their feet could hold out. In the jungle it is a lot wetter than you might think and impossible to keep your feet dry. Jungle boots used to be made of canvas so they got wet but also, theoretically, dried out. But with the constant damp they fell to bits in a few weeks. Then the feet did too.

About the best thing you can do to take care of your feet in the absence of powder is to take your boots off when you rest up and let your feet dry out. This hardens the skin and goes some way to killing the fungus or at least stops it taking hold.

If it is very cold you have frostbite to worry about too. You get this when a bit of your body gets so cold the blood supply stops and the flesh dies. It is quite nasty as the affected part goes black, starts to smell and drops off after gangrene sets in. Try to avoid frostbite. You can walk with frostbitten fingers or nose but frostbite in your feet makes walking hard work. Again, try to keep your feet dry and warm but also avoid boots which are too tight as this partially cuts off blood circulation and encourages your feet to die. Better to wear boots a little too large, and make sure you don't over-pack them by wearing too many extra socks.

## SHELTERS

It's important to know not just how to find or make a shelter, but also when you shouldn't be stopping. Every minute you spend in bandit country increases your chances of getting caught. All it takes is some methodical searcher or an unlucky meeting with a local and you are done for. Dead or rotting in a cell. So what you want to do is make the best speed you can homeward bound without getting careless or so tired that you aren't thinking straight. Here it's a trade-off between making good speed by running as if on exercise but getting too tired to think, and taking your time but increasing the risk of bumping into someone.

If you expect to reach safety, an extraction by air or sea, a friendly border or a base camp within a couple of days, you don't want to be spending time sleeping when you could be moving. On the other hand, it might not be safe to move by day because of the locals or maybe you can't find your way by night.

You should lie up somewhere safe only if you really have to because you are wounded, tired beyond endurance, waiting for extraction or are hiding from the locals. At all other times, you should be making the best speed home that won't leave you so shattered you can't think straight.

Given you need to take shelter for a while, what sort of place to choose? Obviously it depends entirely on the weather, ground and situation, but there are some guidelines I can give you which might make all the difference. The first thing is, you don't make yourself a fancy shelter in the woods or the desert. You make the minimum you need for the job of letting you get a rest. That might mean keeping warm where it is cold, keeping dry (hopefully) where it is wet and keeping out of sight where people are looking for you.

The main thing about your shelter, besides keeping off the sun, wind or rain, is that it should effectively hide you. Certainly from ground observation and, depending on your situation, you might not want to be visible from the air either.

Your shelter must not be on or near any sort of track as this may bring visitors to your door. Any reasonable person should be able to walk right past without noticing you so it doesn't want to stick out like a sore thumb. A useful tip is to find a hollow and level it off with your waterproof and infrared-proof sheet, then cover this with whatever is around – sand, leaves, mud. Creep inside when you are sure you have left no trace of your presence visible.

When you are alone, you cannot have a guard rota. Personally I think a guard rota, or 'stag', is more of a drain on the men than the risk of sleeping when there are only a few men in the team. Of course, with any unit of men, some people need to sleep at their 'stand-to' positions – that is, behind their guns in place to cover their arcs of fire and defend the position. The best way of dealing with this lack of guard is to double back on your path, as for a dog-leg ambush of those following you, and then set up your hide where any pursuers will have to pass it at a safe yet audible distance. This way they will perhaps wake you up without stumbling across you so you have time to either prepare a surprise for them or run away.

## SLEEPING BAG

In cold places, a sleeping bag is the primary way of keeping warm, dry and alive. You will keep yourself warm while you are on the march but as soon as you stop you will begin to cool down. Even in Africa we used to carry lightweight sleeping bags to keep the night chill off. Admittedly, this was because our bodies had become used to the heat but this may well be true for you too. Whenever you stop for more than a moment in cold weather you should get into your bag if you have one. A good sleeping bag is worth its weight in gold and will keep you comfortable and allow you to sleep in the desert, on a mountain or anywhere. Trouble is, you just won't have one, will you?

## INSULATION

The next best thing to a sleeping bag is insulation packed into a big plastic bag or envelope which keeps the wind and rain off. If you don't have a sleeping bag you can make a 'wrap' or envelope out of some plastic sheeting and pack that out with bracken, straw or grass. This can be surprisingly effective and comfortable.

Insulation in your clothing is a long way behind that. You should always wear combat gear which is plenty big enough for you so you can stuff ammo, food or whatever down your jacket front. Looser clothing also makes less of a solid outline and so is easier to camouflage and hide in. This is *much* more important than looking like a smart hero. More important anyway.

What you need to do is collect grass or similar and stuff it inside your trousers and jacket to trap air. This is messy and takes some time but is well worth the trouble when it makes the difference between dying of hypothermia and getting home. If it is available, balled-up newspaper works well but there is never a paper about when you want one.

## FINDING A SHELTER

Like I said, when you want to take shelter, get off the track and out of sight. The place you should pick to take a rest overnight, for the daylight or for several days needs to be a hide more than it needs to be a hotel. If this relates to your situation, beware of caves as the locals will know they are there and search them.

If it is hot, you need shelter from the sun as you will probably be lying up during the day to save water. In a cold climate it is more the wind than the cold that cools you down so you need to think first about getting out of the wind, then the snow, rain or whatever. Very often you cannot help but stay wet but you must get out of that wind or it will kill you. The Inuit, when they live in igloos, have to keep the inside below freezing or it melts, but because there is no wind whatsoever it feels quite warm and comfortable.

## BUILDING A SHELTER

Given you don't have a survival tent which weighs nothing, reflects infrared light, is camouflaged, keeps the wind and rain off and has room service, the next best thing is a plastic sheet.

It is surprisingly difficult to make a roof from grass or leaves that stops the rain and it takes ages so you can't do it anyway. Using a plastic sheet and a bit of cord, it does not take any great DIY skills to make a serviceable shelter and if it happens to be infrared-reflective then you have almost the perfect tent.

I will say it again: the main purpose of a shelter is to keep the wind off. In cold weather it's the wind that kills you. Use your sheet to make a roof too if rain is a pressing problem, but if it is windy make a windbreak with it. Even if the sheet is your only groundsheet and the floor is sodden, you are better off making a bed of leaves and using the sheet to keep the wind off you.

What you can do with it and the choices you make depend a great deal on what you have and what the weather is like but here are a few examples:

In strong wind where hiding is not the priority, you can make a comfortable shelter with just a plastic sheet and some string or bungees (a length of elastic with a hook on each end). If your sheet is big enough, it can keep the wind and rain off and also serve as a groundsheet.

If you are in the open desert, a scrape in the ground may be the best you can do. If you have no sheet, being in a hole will keep the wind off – and it does get cool and breezy in some deserts. If you have a sheet, cover yourself with it. Make a frame to place the sheet on if you have the necessary and then you can also cover it with sand or whatever is about to make it harder to spot.

In snow, you may be lucky and have lots of pine trees. These stop the snow with their branches and it builds up around them to keep the wind off as well. A snow wall makes a surprisingly good insulator and you can spend a reasonable night under the branches of some types of pine tree, particularly if you have a sheet to keep the drips off.

If wind is a problem and there is nowhere to get out of it, you can make a wind-break with a number of stakes and something to weave between them. This may also be used to hide a fire and keep it from burning away too quickly.

# Appendix:
# Your Survival Kit

**B**elow you will find lists of kit which may well come in handy in a survival situation. Take a look through these when you are ready to put together the equipment you need for your next mission. Rather than adopt a 'one size fits all' approach, the idea is that you should mix and match the items to make up the right survival kit for your own situation. I have put items into logical groupings and for some I have added a brief note.

Make sure you have carefully read the whole book before you start trying to choose what you need from these lists. What you should take with you depends on where you are going and what you are doing but most of all it depends on what you can carry. If you take everything, you will need a bullock cart to drag it behind you.

If you find yourself in a difficult situation of the kind we have looked at, you can increase your chances of survival dramatically by owning a little pack of goodies called a survival kit. But the thing I want you to remember about survival kits is that they work best when they are with you rather than back in the sergeants' mess.

Do you have a burglar alarm at home? Do you use it all the time? From a security assessment perspective, I want to tell you that the more complicated an alarm is, and the longer it takes to 'set' when you go out, the fewer times the average person will use it. Because it gets to be just too much trouble. And you will only ever be burgled when the alarm is off. This is a well-known fact in the security industry.

So a person might be better with a simpler alarm which can be set at the touch of a button. Why am I telling you this here, do you think? I am telling you about alarms because I want you to remember that the more trouble your survival kit is to collect and to carry the less you are going to bother taking it with you. And you know damn well the time you will need it is the time it won't be there.

So, when you are putting your kit together, don't overdo it, and keep it somewhere handy so you can clip it to your belt as you go. Better still, keep it clipped to your belt – not in your pack.

I can't tell you precisely which of these items you need to keep in your kit as this depends on where you are in the world, the job you are doing and, not least, your usual form of transport. If you are walking, weight is obviously more of an issue than if you are a flyboy or a tanky. Let's just take a look at the options and then, after considering the pros and cons as they apply to your mission, you can mix and match as you think best.

## FIGHTING EQUIPMENT

This is what you hope to be left with after you have lost your pack and rifle. The only thing you are at a disadvantage with is range and hitting power of the pistol compared with your rifle, and if you don't have a .45 you have to get up close with any pistol and go for a head shot. Two in the head and you know that he's dead.

### PISTOL

A revolver doesn't jam but is slow to reload and, as it is slightly fatter than an automatic pistol, not so good for hiding on the body. Automatic pistols have a higher rate of fire and are slimmer. The small-calibre .22-inch pistol is a small weapon, easy to hide and carry ammo for but only stops a man with a head shot. The .38 revolver and 9mm pistol are a little underpowered and require a head shot to be sure of a kill. The .45 revolver and automatic pistols are big weapons with small magazines but they do disable or kill with one shot to the body. The .38 Special, which is a .38 with a longer case and a bigger propellant charge, is a good compromise for the revolver. The 9mm Beretta is a very good automatic with a 13-round magazine.

### GRENADES

Grenades are so useful you should never be without at least a few. I sometimes carry twelve for close combat. Shrapnel grenades of any kind are the best to carry for general escape and evasion use as they are ideal for slowing pursuit, clearing crowds and bars and making booby-traps. Day or night, grenades do not give your position away.

### KNIFE

A lot of guys get all gung-ho about fancy knives and think they make you a hero. Actually you can kill with a neck cut using the tiniest penknife or box-cutter. For choice, a fighting knife needs to be 15cm (6 inches) long to penetrate the chest and deep enough to make a big wound so that the target bleeds to death quickly. Avoid a knife which is too long or heavy to move quickly. A double-edged weapon is probably the favourite for fighting an opponent but if you get close enough to fight with a knife you are probably doing something wrong.

It makes sense to have one knife double as a weapon and a tool for cutting food and sticks, so some compromise is a good idea. A knife with a saw blade on the back makes it much easier to cut stakes for use in a shelter or booby-trap. As a weapon, a knife does not need to be very sharp as the point will enter the body under only finger and thumb pressure, but to cut meat, food and other things it is best sharp. It takes a great deal of practice to sharpen a knife with a stone or 'steel' sharpener, so go to a good hardware shop and get yourself a proprietary sharpener with rolling discs that set the edge correctly.

### HEAT-REFLECTIVE SHEET/OVERALLS

If the opposition might come looking for you with infrared equipment, it is a really good idea to be wearing overalls which break up the body's heat signature. Even better, get yourself a large sheet of material which reflects infrared and blocks the heat from your own body. You can hide under this when a chopper is overhead and it should double as a rainproof sheet to make a shelter with.

## MEDICAL EQUIPMENT

What you need to do is read a good book on emergency medical treatment such as is written for explorers or long-distance sailors. Then get yourself on a medical course so you know how to use the kit.

Some of what I list here is not easily available to civilians yet is issued as a matter of course to special forces. If you are in the forces, have a word with your medical officer or doctor, because if you have the training they are more likely to hand over what you want.

### BROAD-SPECTRUM ANTIBIOTIC

If you get a cut or wound, take a course of antibiotics to kill the infection. Better safe than sorry. Make sure you finish the course of pills, whether it lasts days or weeks, or they won't work.

### SUTURES

Anything more than a shaving cut needs stitching up with a suture. This slows the bleeding and lets the blood clot while holding the edges of the skin and flesh together so that they can heal. You could, theoretically, stitch a wound with a needle and cotton but there would be massive infection, so only do this if you are desperate and the casualty is going to see a doctor soon. Fortunately, a suture is cleverer than that. Each suture comes as a length of special line with a sort of barbless fishing hook on the end. Some sutures are made to dissolve in the body in a few weeks, while others are not. With the dissolving kind you can fasten the edges of deep muscle cuts together before doing the surface, in the knowledge that the stitches will disappear. If you have to use a non-dissolving suture, when the wound is healed enough not to open, you will need to cut each stitch where it comes out of the skin and slide them out individually.

The easiest way to stitch a wound is to use a pair of tweezers to hold the hook and keep it sterile while you pass it through the pieces of flesh and tie off each stitch. Disinfect the wound first and don't touch the 'thread'. Try to get the flaps on the flesh straight and lined up or when they heal it will leave a lumpy, twisted scar. This is easier than it sounds, though of course it's tricky to get someone to let you practise.

### PAINKILLERS
You can get painkillers from the chemist but for something stronger you need to see the medics. You can still work with strong painkillers and think clearer without the pain.

### MORPHINE INJECTOR
Morphine is a strong painkiller for serious wounds. It will put the recipient out of action so don't use it on yourself if you have to walk, think or fight. Do not give morphine for a head injury. Very often morphine comes in a little injector package and you can tape this to the cord on your dog tags.

CRAPPING PILLS

If you have dysentery, or the shits really bad, you will be losing fluid very quickly and this can put you out of action or even kill you. There are pills which stop this. If you have been eating just meat for some time, you may not be crapping at all. There are pills which will sort this too – sometimes with amusing results.

WAKING PILLS/SLEEPING PILLS

I have never needed sleeping pills and most soldiers I know of are so knackered they can sleep on a washing line. What you may need is waking pills. There are stimulants which the medics can give you to keep you alert and awake for days. If you were holding a position against constant assault, you might need something like this. Or if you had to keep walking for days to make an RV. When you have been awake for a few days you start to hallucinate, which is good for a laugh but not so good when you are working. Use them with discretion.

K PILLS

There are many names for sugar pills but they all give you a quick shot of glucose which will keep you running a bit longer. We have always called them K pills on the grounds that they will keep you going for another kilometre. The idea is that the body can use the sugar quickly for a boost. Bread or pasta is better for stamina so eat toast before a long march.

SALT

If you are sweating a lot, you are losing salt. In warm countries this can be serious and along with your water you should take salt tablets to make up the loss. They usually have minerals and vitamins in too so they must be good for you.

### SALINE DRIP

There are lots of different blood groups, as you probably know. If someone loses a lot of blood, they may die before the body can replace it. Like a car running low on coolant. A quick fix for blood loss and severe shock, both of which withdraw blood to the core organs, is a saline drip. This is a bag full of salt water and minerals which you feed into the body through a tube. Slide the needle into a vein such as inside the elbow, then clear the bubbles from the tube – they can kill if they get to the brain – by running the fluid and flicking on the flow-speed control on the tube. Raise the bag, connect the tube to the needle and set the flow speed. Even if you cannot get a medic, you have just improved your mate's chances.

### WOUND-DRESSING KIT

For all the little cuts and bruises you get at kindergarten, you need a set of dressings and the know-how to apply them:
- Scissors for trimming dressings and bandages.
- Tweezers for removing small objects such as splinters.
- Thermometer to check for fever or infection etc.
- Sterilised pads for use as dressings.
- Large dressings for serious wounds, to control bleeding and prevent infection.
- Safety pins for securing the ends of bandages and slings.

- Pack of plasters for minor wounds, cuts and blisters.
- Triangular bandages for use folded as a bandage, opened out as a sling, or as dressing for large wounds.
- Adhesive micro-tape for securing dressings and bandages.

## HUNTING AND COOKING EQUIPMENT

### MATCHES

Waxed matches survive well and you know at a glance that they have not run out. A cigarette lighter may run out without you noticing, though it is the easiest way to light a fire.

### MAGNIFYING GLASS

In a sunny climate and daylight, it is very easy to light some tinder with a magnifying glass and they weigh nothing.

### WATER CARRIERS

You should have two water bottles on your belt and another two in your pack. Besides this, it is always a good idea to carry the fold-flat type somewhere you won't get separated from them. You will only need to get really thirsty once to remember this and make it a priority.

### WATER-STERILISATION PILLS

Always put sterilisation pills in water before you drink it, especially in hot countries as there are more bugs. You will only forget to do this once if you get a good bug. If a bug puts you out of action when you are on the run, you are likely to die.

### SNARES

A snare is a wire noose made of slightly springy wire. Wire is used so the animal you trap cannot bite through it and escape. It's not a humane way to hunt but better than starving. Set snares on animal tracks and catch tasty, furry critters every night.

### FISHING EQUIPMENT

A length of line with a baited hook on the end can mean the difference between a nice fish supper and not having the strength to march the next day. Tie the line so there is a weight at the end and the hook is on a side-branch 30–60cm (1–2 feet) before the end. This lets you throw the line where you want it and, when you get a fish on, you just haul it straight in without the weight swinging the line around and tangling. For bait, use a bit of bread, cheese, meat or a bug, or, if none of these is available, a bit of silver paper or bright plastic will attract fish to the hook.

### COOKING POT

A luxury, I know, but if you can carry one or find one it makes cooking so much easier and stewed rat is such a pleasant change from roasted rat. You can have boiled veg with it too.

### SPOON

Anything boiled in a can is far easier to eat if you have a spoon.

## TREATS

Meat tastes bloody awful without salt and salt is good for you whatever the health Gestapo say. Take a little salt for adding to the meat, and a little curry powder makes the most disgusting things go down easily. Both weigh nothing.

## SHELTER-MAKING EQUIPMENT

### PLASTIC SHEETS

A plastic sheet is the most versatile and useful item of survival equipment you can get. Best if it is camouflaged and stops infrared but even a sheet of polythene is great. You can make a ridge tent to keep the rain off, a groundsheet to keep out the wet below you, a windbreak to keep the wind-chill from killing you, and, wrapped round you and packed with grass, it even makes a sleeping bag. If you are making one up at home, put in some eyelets all round the edges so the cord or bungees don't tear out.

### CORD/BUNGEES

Cord is handy for making tents and a thousand other things, while bungees don't tangle and are quick to stow. I prefer cord but some prefer bungees.

### SLEEPING BAG

A sleeping bag with a built-in groundsheet is all you need in almost any weather to stay snug, dry and warm. You can take off wet clothes and boots then dry them with your body heat inside. This is a luxury, though, and the chances are you will not be able to carry such a thing. Unless you are tank crew.

### THERMAL BLANKET

A thermal, survival or 'silver', blanket is made of a shiny foil stuck to a stronger backing. It is paper-thin, almost weightless, stops the wind and reflects body heat very well, so when covered by one the body gets warm in moments. Many double as waterproof covers. They are handy for wrapping someone who has hypothermia but at a push will double as an easy-to-carry sleeping bag.

## NAVIGATION AND SOS SIGNALLING EQUIPMENT

### RADIO

If you still have your radio, you can call for a taxi – unless anyone on the other side is listening or looking to trace your call. Keep calls brief and plan what you are going to say first. You may have to get anyone who replies (any good guys anyway) to pass on a message.

### MOBILE PHONE

A mobile phone may not work for calls where you are but when switched on it can be traced. So, as long as the opposition don't have the gear, leave your phone on for your signals people to locate you.

SATELLITE PHONE

A satellite phone will send or receive a message from anywhere. They are still a little hefty at the moment, but doubtless they will get smaller and lighter, like most high-tech kit.

RADIO DISTRESS BEACON

Yachting people all have access to survival beacons which are triggered when dunked in the sea. You can get yourself something similar and set it off when things go wrong.

GPS

Knowing where you are is half the battle when it comes to getting home. Not only does a GPS system tell you where you are *and* help to guide you home, but many also have built-in radio distress beacons.

COMPASS

Learn to use a compass well and with this tiny piece of unbreakable kit you can find your way across a continent. At the very least you can save a lot of boot leather.

MAP

A map might be an Ordnance Survey chart showing individual buildings or it might be drawn in crayon and show just the highway and a river, but any map is better than none. If you have an idea of where you are and where you want to be, with a map and some way of finding North, you are on the right track.

TORCH

There is no point having a map and not being able to see it when you are travelling at night. Hand-cranked torches don't need batteries but for survival use their size and weight are a drawback. The best thing is a tiny torch and a fresh battery.

FLARES

The best way to attract attention, bar none, is a rocket flare. They shoot up into the sky and burst in lovely colours, telling everyone for miles around where you are. If you are going to use a rocket flare, and they are great for signalling ships, make sure you know both that the colours you are going to use and the flares won't light up until they are high enough not to give your position away. Hand-held flares make a very bright light for long enough for a boat or sub to know where you are. Again, PPPPPP: Proper Planning Prevents Piss-Poor Performance.

## SUGGESTED SURVIVAL KIT

Here is the basic survival kit I recommend. You will probably either see it as too much to carry or a list to get you started.

Pistol
Grenades
Map
Compass
Small torch
Antibiotics
Painkillers

Sutures
Wound dressings
Plastic sheet with eyelets and infrared-proof
15 metres (50 feet) of cord
Waxed matches
Knife with saw blade
Fishing line and hooks
Snares
Water-sterilisation pills
Water bottles (preferably flat-pack)
Radio distress beacon